Grov

A Rather Special Place
Growing Up in Cardiff Dockland

Winn Anderson

GOMER

First Impression—1993

ISBN 0 86383 861 8

© Winn Anderson

Printed by J.D. Lewis and Sons Ltd., Gomer Press, Llandysul, Dyfed.

In grateful memory of
my husband

ACKNOWLEDGEMENTS

I would like to thank the following for providing photographs and giving permission for them to be reproduced:

Alan Goldsworthy and family for the portrait of Lydia Evans. (Photo: Adrian Goldsworthy.)

The present Lewis Dawkin-Jones for *The Rajore*.

Welsh Industrial & Maritime Museum for the pilot cutters.

Kevin Counsell for the Royal Exchange.

Mr and Mrs Albert Ley for Whitsun Treat pictures.

Mrs Ethel Willie for picture of James Buck.

I am also very grateful to my son for his hard work in editing my manuscript and generally getting the book ready for publication; for checking facts and for locating and obtaining the photographs; without his enthusiasm the book would never have been finished.

While all the characters in this book are or were real people, some names have been changed.

CHAPTER 1

They called him 'the Stormy Petrel'. He was a Bristol Channel pilot about a hundred years ago. Imagine him—a beautiful-looking man with white hair blowing in the wind, a long beard, deep dark grey eyes and a Grecian nose—standing, one foot on the gunwale of his little punt, the other on the rope ladder of some great sailing ship; waiting, perfectly balanced, as the boat sways and dips beneath him, for just the right moment to start climbing. Yet he cannot swim a stroke.

He is dressed, summer and winter, in a formal and expensive bespoke suit, a watchchain across the waistcoat—never a hat or topcoat—and under his arm a package of gospel tracts for the captain and crew.

His name was Peter Evans and he was my grandfather. He was generous and impulsive, quick-tempered, fearless—and a true eccentric.

One day he went to a funeral. Funerals then were not made so easy as they are nowadays. The men followed the hearse on foot, often for several miles. On this occasion Peter was wearing a new pair of boots which his wife, Liza, had ordered for him. As always they were hand-made in the best quality soft leather. But this particular pair pinched. The walk to the church was a long one, and so was the service. Then came the further walk to the cemetery. Before starting on that, however, my grandfather removed his boots, deposited them in the gutter, and went the rest of the way in his socks. I hope those boots were found by someone who needed them.

In case you have decided that Peter Evans was just a silly old man, of whom you have already had enough, let me correct that impression by telling of the time that a foreign ship arrived in Cardiff with a sailor on board suffering from smallpox. He was isolated in his cabin and nobody—not his own captain, nor shipmates, nor doctors, nor nurses—would go to him. In those days smallpox was usually fatal.

My grandfather went to the sick man's cabin, picked him up and carried him to his own pilot cutter, which he had moored alongside.

Peter Evans, 'the Stormy Petrel'.

For six weeks he remained with that sailor, nursing him back to health. During that time he saw none of his family and must have lost a great deal of money. But it was all in a day's work. He didn't want thanks. Someone had had to do it. He did it.

My family lived in the docklands of Cardiff. When I say this many people will assume that I am talking about Butetown—the notorious 'Tiger Bay'. In fact, our district was quite a distance from Tiger Bay, and a very different kind of neighbourhood.

Going south from the centre of Cardiff, you eventually come to Bute Road. As you travel down it the docks are to your left. For the first mile Tiger Bay used to be to your right. (It has now been replaced by high-rise flats.) Then you find yourself skirting the commercial area centred on Mountstuart Square—a region of large and imposing Victorian office buildings, housing coal exporters, ship owners and the Exchange, as well as banks, solicitors, accountants and so on. When I was young and Cardiff was the busiest coal-exporting port in the world there was great wealth and great activity here, the floor of the Coal Exchange as crowded with dealers as that of the London Stock Exchange.

Still continuing south, beyond the commercial district, you come (or came, for again they have all been flattened to make way for new council houses) to Docklands, usually shortened to just 'the Docks', an area of small working-class homes occupied largely by people who were considered more 'respectable' than the inhabitants of Butetown. No doubt this was highly unfair to many of the Tiger Bay residents, though the fact remains that my sisters and I thought nothing of walking through the Docks at night, while we would have been very dubious about doing this in Butetown.

Royal Exchange, Mount Stuart Square.

11

Bute Esplanade.

Beyond these small houses again were several esplanades of three or four-storey Victorian terraced houses, some overlooking the Bristol Channel. These homes were occupied by port officials, shipping office staff, the local doctors, the schoolmaster, the vicar, retired sea captains, pilots and the like. Nowadays they are considered of great architectural value, Bute Esplanade being referred to in an article in the *South Wales Echo* as 'a nineteenth century gem in the heart of Cardiff docklands, which would be an asset to any city'; while a year or two ago an attempt was made to have the streets Bute and Windsor Esplanades and Bute Terrace designated a conservation area.

It was in No. 4 Bute Esplanade that Peter Evans, the Stormy Petrel, lived with his wife and children. Immediately opposite the house was a small, locked Corporation garden, with lawns and flower beds, and beyond that a great sea wall, four feet high, against which the spring tides would beat.

There were eventually nine Evans children: five boys and four girls. Something of the Stormy Petrel was in each of them. They were

12

brilliant, eccentric, erratic. There was, moreover, a vein of tragedy in the family.

The eldest son, Peter, followed his father into the merchant marine, qualified as a chief engineer at a very early age and then one day mysteriously went to his cabin and shot himself. The second, George, also a pilot and a superb swimmer, was on board a ship which foundered quite close to land. Men were taking to the boats, but George didn't bother; he decided to swim ashore. He dived overboard. As he broke surface the anchor was dropped. It struck him on the head, killing him instantly. Another son, Yant, had a heart attack while pushing his car after a breakdown in London. And the youngest, Henry—incredibly energetic, bursting with ideas, generous and highly emotional—was a brilliant businessman, who made a fortune, lost it, and then made another one.

Peter and Liza with their children.

13

Of the daughters, Bessie was among the first generation of college girls. She would have been, I suppose, one of the original bluestockings. She qualified as a teacher and eventually became a headmistress. A stern and forbidding figure, for whom everything and everybody had to be just so, she was always held rather in awe. The next daughter, Annie, married a Scottish businessman, lived to be over ninety, took—and loved—her first flight when she was well into her eighties, and a few months before she died was seen running for a bus.

Raising such a large family was an expensive business for Peter and Liza Evans, and they were moreover great entertainers. Fortunately, my grandfather made good money. He would come in from work, tell Liza to hold out the skirt of her long black dress, and then would toss into it handfuls of golden sovereigns from his pockets.

The money would soon be spent. Saturday morning was Liza's shopping time. Every week at nine o'clock her regular cabby, a man called Harry Smith, would arrive to convey her to town. First he would take her to one of the big Cardiff department stores—James Howell, David Morgan or Samuel Hall—for whatever she needed in the way of clothes, linens, materials, china and so on. Then it would be on to the Central Market for the weekly food purchases. One stall would sell only butter and cheese. There might be half a dozen huge slabs of different kinds of butter, covered with muslin. The stall holder would cut little bits off each slab, put them on a small white scrubbed board and pass it to her to sample. She would make her decision and buy a great twelve or fourteen pound block.

Then she would pass on to the butcher's stall, where she would purchase several huge joints of meat, whole hams, pounds of liver. The butcher, Mr Richards, did his own slaughtering and was always particularly proud of this. 'Lovely this week, Mrs Ivvans,' he would invariably say, 'Richards's own liver.' Harry Smith would meanwhile be carrying the purchases back to the cab and loading up.

When she had finished and it was time for Harry to take her home, there would hardly be enough room for Liza in the cab.

I can remember only one of my great-grandparents, and that is Grandma Davies—Liza's mother. My recollection of her is, I must admit, rather vague, as she was already an old lady when I was a toddler. But I do have memory of a tiny woman who looked like a typical grandmother in an old-fashioned picture book, wearing a long black dress, with a white fichu at the neck and a little white cap.

Although I have little personal remembrance of her, because of the stories my mother told me about her, I have always felt that I knew her well. She was apparently a remarkable peson, a woman of boundless energy who, over many years, developed what was, for those days, a really marvellous knowledge of medicine. It was quite impossible then (the first half of the nineteenth century) for a woman to qualify as a doctor, but certainly Grandma Davies did the next best thing. I suppose her system was a combination of conventional medicine, learnt from such books as she could get hold of, folk remedies and herbalism. (The only thing that really concerned her about any treatment was whether it worked.) But I suspect the most important element was a natural gift.

In that period, for the poor a doctor was a luxury. Doctors had to be paid on the spot; and although some doctors would give their services free to the really needy, generally speaking if the money wasn't available the sick just had to suffer. However, as Grandma's reputation grew—first within the family, then among immediate friends, and gradually around the neighbourhood—it wasn't long before, when anyone fell ill, the call would go out: 'Sent for Mrs Davies.' And Grandma would go—any time, day or night.

Her fame was probably sealed when one night about three o'clock there came a frantic hammering on the front door. The visitor turned out to be a very distraught woman.

'Oh, ma'am,' she gasped, 'could you come and look at our Joe? He's in a terrible way. I—I think he's dying.'

A few minutes later Grandma was following her through the dark streets. One the way the woman poured out the story. The boy had been ill for some time, with a high fever, headaches, aching limbs and a sore throat. Suddenly tonight he had got much worse. He couldn't breathe. He seemed to be choking.

Grandma's heart sank. The symptoms sounded horribly ominous

The woman led her to a small terraced house and upstairs to a back bedroom. In the bed lay a little boy. He was breathing in tiny, short gasps, fighting for every breath. Around the bed, staring helplessly, some of them in tears, were four or five other children.

Grandma hurried across to the bed and raised the boy up. She felt his forehead, then tilting his head back, ordered sharply: 'Bring that lamp over here—as close as you can.'

By the still inadequate light she peered down the boy's throat. Her worst fears were realized. It was diphtheria.

The modern generation will perhaps not realize what a scourge diphtheria was in those says. Most children who contracted it died, death being caused by the formation of a tough membrane across the throat, bringing asphyxiation.

Grandma turned to the mother. 'Take those children out of here at once,' she said briskly.

As the woman complied, Grandma stood, looking down at the boy. It was quite obvious he could not go on like this. Every second his breathing was becoming more laboured. He would be dead in minutes, from suffocation—unless she took drastic action. There was only one thing she could think to do. But dare she risk it? She hestitated for only a few seconds. She knew she had no choice.

Grandma said a little prayer, tilted the boy's head back as far as it would go and thrust her hand into his mouth. By now he was choking and purple in the face. She heard the mother, coming back into the room, give a gasp of horror. But Grandma was forcing her fingers right down into the boy's throat. At last they met the hard, leathery obstruction. She managed to grip it between her forefinger and thumb. Then she closed her eyes and jerked with all her might.

The membrane came away. The boy gave a screech of pain. It was echoed by his mother. Grandma gazed down at him. It was miraculous. Already he was taking great gasps of air, his chest heaving; and his colour was returning to normal.

The mother whispered: 'Is—is he all right?'

'I think he's going to be. He will be in a great deal of pain with his throat, but that will heal. He must take only liquids—milk, broth, gruel. And tomorrow I will bring around a mixture of my own, with which he must gargle.'

She cut short the woman's attempt at incoherent thanks. 'To see him well again is all the thanks I want. Now, about your other children. You must keep them away from him.' If, she thought to herself, it's not already too late.

16

But on this occasion her fears were groundless. Amazingly, none of the other children contracted the disease. And the boy, after several painful weeks, made a complete recovery.

After this incident, Grandma Davies could do no wrong in the neighbourhood. In time she became universally known as the Docks'

The author's great grandmother Davies ('the Docks' Doctor'), sitting, with her daughter Liza Evans, right, Liza's daughter Bess, and Bess's baby.

Doctor, and her tiny figure, in bonnet and cloak, scurrying from house to house, became one of the most familiar sights in the district.

She made only two real rules. She always told people that, while she would do what she could, if she came up against anything really serious and was unable to help, she would tell them so. And, of course, she never took a penny in payment.

I wish I could end this story by saying that people turned up in hundreds for her funeral, but I just don't remember ever having been told anything about it. I cannot even say when she died. I do know that her legend, as they say, lived on for many a year.

★   ★   ★

The Evanses were staunch Christians, members of the religious group known to outsiders as the Plymouth Brethren, but who preferred to call themselves simply Brethren. In those early days the Brethren had no local church and used to meet and hold their services in a variety of places: a schoolroom; a room over a stable; and for a time a deserted hospital ship. Their first really permanent place of worship was known as the Old Sea Lock Hall, and was a small meeting house just beyond the old Glamorganshire Canal, the mouth of which was about half a mile from my grandparents' home. The church could afford no organ, but the Evanses owned a harmonium and each Sunday they would wheel this through the streets to the hall. The most difficult part must have been manoeuvring it over the narrow lock footbridge, though on one bitingly cold winter Sunday the canal was covered with such a thick layer of ice that they were able to slide the harmonium across.

Later, in 1899, a fine new church, the Ebenezer Gospel Hall, seating some five hundred, was built a mile or two away, in the Grangetown district. Ebenezer was to play an enormous part in the life of my family.

Peter Evans was one of the first Superintendents of the Sunday School, which used to be held in the basement. When he talked to the children he would pace from side to side, occasionally pausing to stand with his foot on the fender of the big open fireplace. However, one of the more tiresome members of the church, a Mr Massie, decided that this was undignified and suggested that the Superintendent should have a platform or dais, from which to speak. After consideration, my grandfather turned this idea down. To express himself freely, he said, he had to be able to move around. A few weeks later, he arrived on a Sunday afternoon to find a brand new portable wooden rostrum at the far end of the room, right in the centre. Grandfather snorted, dragged it bodily to one side and carried on as before. Nothing was said by Massie or my grandfather. But the next week the rostrum was out in front again. Once more grandfather heaved it to the side. When on the third Sunday he found the thing again in position his temper snapped. Lifting the rostrum in both hands he hurled it against the wall, breaking it in several pieces. That was the end of the matter.

No, he was no meek and mild Christian. But he was unswerving and fearless in his conviction, and made a tremendous impression on everyone with whom he came in contact. He died eventually at the age of seventy-six, dropping down dead in the street. As he would have wished, he died with his boots on. Unless he had already taken them off and thrown them away.

Looking back, my grandfather seems in every way a larger than life person. Would he, though, have seemed so at the time? It appears to me that there were many more 'characters' about in those days. For instance, there were people like Mr Spencer, who made a point of walking in front of the new-fangled tram cars, refusing to move aside because he had been there first; and who, when set upon and punched by a drunken tough in the street, deliberately turned the other cheek to him. The drunk punched that one too. Whereupon Mr Spencer said: 'That's all my Lord told me to do,' and proceeded to give the drunk a good hiding.

Then there was old James Buck, the headmaster of the local school, who, when displeased by a pupil, had been known to throw the miscreant downstairs—then hurl the mat on top of him. Parents, however, never complained, the pupils did not seem any the worse, and all left thoroughly competent in reading, writing and arithmetic.

It was James Buck who had preceeded my grandfather as Sunday School Superintendent; and on his completion of twenty-five years' service, it fell to my grandfather, as senior teacher, to present him

James Buck.

with a heavy black marble clock, to mark the occasion. Fifty years later I was to marry James Buck's grandson. And more than fifty years after that, the clock is still ticking merrily away on our mantelpiece.

Next door but one to Peter and Liza Evans lived their friends, William and Anne Jones, with their four sons. Later the second Jones son, Lewis, was to marry Lydia, the third Evans daughter. They became my parents.

William Jones, like Peter Evans, was a pilot and also white-bearded; but in every other respect was the complete opposite to his friend. He was reliable, predictable, his feet firmly on the ground—a nice man.

(I naturally describe both my grandfathers as they looked in later life, which is how I remember them. Unfortunately, the only photographs that survive show them as comparatively young men.)

The Bristol Channel has the second highest rise and fall of tide in the world, and its pilots were described in a recent TV programme* as 'genius seamen' and their occupation as 'greatly revered'. According to the Welsh Industrial and Maritime Museum, they were the 'aristocrats' of the Bristol Channel. They sailed as far as the south coast of

*'Under Sail—the Bristol Channel Pilot Cutters'—BBC2

William and Anne Jones with their four sons. Lewis on right.

21

Ireland and fifty miles south of Land's End in search of 'clients'. They were in constant competition for work, always alert for rumours of impending arrivals and then racing each other to reach the approaching ship first. The pilot with the fastest cutter, therefore, had an obvious advantage.

Those cutters were really wonderful craft. In the same TV programme it was said that they were 'one of the sturdiest and best-founded class of boat ever built in Britain' and possessed 'a design which was as near perfect and seaworthy as could possibly be'. Three of them were taken on polar expeditions by the explorer, Major Bill Tilman, who sailed one round the coast of Africa and South America to the Antarctic. Another, built in Cardiff, still sails along the coast of Holland today.

Pilot Cutter *Spray*.

(Welsh Ind. & M. Mus)

Pilot Cutters' Race, 1903.

They were fifty feet long, so below deck there was room for a saloon, with sleeping bunks, a galley and storage compartments. In 1902 it cost £400 to have one built. (Recently one was valued at £30,000!) The crew would usually consist of a man and a boy—often the pilot's son. A punt, or small dinghy, would be carried, and when the pilot was within hailing distance of a big ship and confirmed that his services were required, the boy would row him across and then return to the cutter. Sometimes, however, the cutter would be towed home behind the ship. This saved the pilot the delay of waiting in port, after docking, for his cutter to arrive; on the other hand, it was tiring and difficult work keeping the cutter under control in the wake of a large, fast-moving ship.

Payment was according to the size of the ship—£7 being an average charge for a craft of 25,000 tons. (Today it is in the region of £150.)

Each year there would be a Review Day when the boats had to fit out for inspection. Afterwards there would be races. My Grandpa

Jones won on several occasions in his cutter, 'The Alfred and William'. He was convinced it was the best pilot cutter on the Bristol Channel, let alone in Cardiff docks; but then, as he used to say: 'I wouldn't give a fig for a man who didn't think his wife was the best wife and his boat was the best boat.'

Of his wife, Anne, I remember very little, except that she seemed always to be reading, usually thrillers or detective stories—presumably among them, though before my time, the first Sherlock Holmes mysteries. She was still reading them, without glasses, when she was well into her eighties. On his retirement, Grandpa and Grandma Jones bought a small house with a large garden. Here they raised chickens—or fowls, as they called them. My brother, sister and I used to visit them every Saturday morning. As soon as we arrived Grandma would fetch the biscuit barrel and give us a ginger biscuit each, and then later on we'd each be allowed to take a fresh, warm egg from the coop—a great thrill, this—or pick or pull something from whatever was in season in the garden.

My father was born in March, 1868, and very early in his life had a burning desire to go to sea. His parents tried to talk him out of it, but he wouldn't be dissuaded, and in November 1882, at the age of fourteen years and eight months, he sailed from Cardiff's East Dock as a cabin boy in the full-rigged ship, 'The Eagle'. Within twenty-four hours he was wishing he was back home but, as he wrote, there are no back doors in ships, and he wasn't to see his parents again for more than sixteen months.

Many years later he produced a book of reminiscences and I think it is well worth quoting from it at some length.

CHAPTER 2

'When I was but eight months past my fourteenth birthday I expressed a wish to go to sea. My father, who was a Bristol Channel pilot, advised me otherwise, but like boys often are at that age, I thought I knew better and so in November 1882 I sailed as a cabin boy in a full-rigged ship, named *The Eagle* from the East Dock, Cardiff.

'I soon learned that my father knew better than I, for within twenty-four hours I wished I was back at home . . .

'When we got to the Equator the men asked the Captain for permission to shave those on board (I think there were six of us) who had never crossed the Line before. The eldest man in the ship—a coloured man—was chosen to act as Neptune. A huge water tub—used for washing decks—was filled with water, all ready for business. Five of those who were to be shaved had already been locked in the carpenter's workshop, ready to be marched out, one by one, by two of the sailors dressed like policemen, but they couldn't find me, the Captain having hidden me in the storeroom, down under the cabin. The men, thinking the Captain was hiding me, marched aft, and knocking at the cabin door Neptune said, "We arrest the boy Lewis in the name of Her Majesty the Queen".

'The Captain, laughing, said, "Bring the boy up, steward," and as I passed him he whispered, "Don't open your mouth." I didn't know what he meant, but I was soon to learn.

'They marched me forrard and sat me on a line stretched across this large tub of water—an apprentice standing each side of the tub, one on each end of the line, so that at the nod of the barber, when he had finished lathering me with a mixture of tar, paint, etc., and scraped a little of it off with a piece of hoop-iron, the boys would step off the line and down I floundered into the tub. Before this was done, the barber began to ask me questions, and immediately I remembered the Captain's advice and opened not my mouth, and presently I found myself down in the water, and two sailors from the top of the half deck were pouring water over me. I learned afterwards that if I had answered their questions they would have pushed a wad of this lather into my mouth. The others in their simplicity had answered to their sorrow . . .

'It was a troublesome passage out—we were bound to Coquimbo, West Coast of South America. We had a very mixed crew, Negroes, Germans, Greeks, Austrians, Italians, English, Irish, Scotch and Welsh, made up our crew of 32, and as a result there were many serious fights on board, sometimes belaying pins and knives being used.

'We arrived at the dreaded Cape Horn, and I shall never forget the buffeting we had for six weeks. The old ship *Eagle*—a wooden ship —had seen the best of her days, and day after day it was pump or sink. Sometimes the men would be washed from the pumps by the seas breaking over us. One day I was in the fore end of the ship and thought I could get aft between the seas, but one caught me, and they thought I was gone overboard, but the Lord preserved me and they found me up against the booby hatch, bruised and shaken. I was soon alright, but such an icy bath is not soon forgotten.

'During those weeks off Cape Horn, we spoke to a fine barque called the *Granville*, and a few days after we had a very bitter gale. Our Captain never expected the old ship to weather that storm. Well, in the mercy of God, we did, but the barque 'Granville' was never heard of again.

'During those weeks of exceptional cold, snow and ice, the old coloured seaman who had acted as Neptune, when we crossed the Equator, was frostbitten in both feet. The Captain had sea-boots for sale in his cabin chest (usually known among sailors as the slop chest), but as they were thirty shillings a pair, and not very good at that, and seeing the money for a sailor was only £2.10s a month, the old sailor would not buy them, but wore his usual "bluchers", with the result I have stated. I must not dwell on the sufferings of that poor man till we arrived at Coquimbo.

'There were no docks there then, and we had to lie out in the stream to anchor. The chief mate took him ashore to a hospital, and both feet were amputated . . . We lay there at anchor four months, two of which we were discharging and two waiting orders. At the end of four months the sailor was brought on board, because no mailboats called at Coqauimbo, but did call at Valpariaiso, to which port we had been ordered.

'When we left Cardiff, the Captain had brought away with him about £100 worth of clothing, boots, etc., with the intention of making a great profit both from the sailors and at the ports to which he was bound. After we had been in port a few days, the Captain called me into the cabin, and as I was tall for my age, now 15 years old, he made me put on two each of underclothing and a suit of clothes, and that is the way, several times, he smuggled the clothes ashore to a Scotsman in Conquimbo who had a small drinking saloon. The saloon keeper's wife gave me a lovely walking stick, made from a whale's jawbone, which I have to this day . . . Such gains did not do the Captain much good, because when we arrived at Valparaiso he was discharged for drunkenness, and the chief mate of a sister ship at Valparaiso was made Captain of the *Eagle*.

The Chancellor, for such was the other ship's name, was loaded with Guano, having loaded it up at the islands called by that name, but had turned back, leaking badly, three times, was condemned, and we had to lash our ship alongside her and take in her cargo, to bring it to St Nazaire, France. I might add that was the last voyage the old *Eagle* made—afterwards becoming a hulk for holding coals . . .

'I have refrained from writing about the conduct of the crew. In each port they were given 48 hours leave and certain money from the Captain; that is, if they had any due to them. After four and a half's months on a passage they usually went on a spree and often got locked up for being drunk and disorderly. The men had been so long without intoxicating drink that a little upset them. I have often seen supposed gentlemen looking with disdain on a drunken sailor, and I knew at the same time that they drank more whisky in a week than the sailor had in months—but they had got used to it. I am glad to say that we have a different class of seamen today—I mean as to sobriety.

'I arrived home from St Nazaire in a French tramp steamer, paying 60 francs for the passage to Cardiff, which we did in the good time of 36 hours. My mother was making bread at the time. I can see even now her face as I entered the kitchen, and her look of astonishment as she saw the boy who had grown 6 inches in sixteen months. Regard-

Lewis Dawkin Jones, aged eighteen.

less of the fact that I had on a black suit, she threw her arms around me and almost spoiled my black coat with flour. What a welcome!'

My father arrived home on 2nd April, 1884 and two days later was apprenticed to his father, with the object of becoming a pilot. His elder brother, Bill, was at that time half way through *his* apprenticeship. Part of their duty was to ferry their father to the ships he had to bring in and then to sail the pilot cutter home. On the shorter journeys just one of the boys would go. There was a tiny galley on the *Alfred & William* and my grandmother would give them hampers of food which simply had to be warmed up. My father recalled once, when he alone had accompanied his father, the hamper contained a huge roly-poly pudding, wrapped in a muslin cloth. 'Come along, my boy,' grandfather said, when he unwrapped it, 'you and I'll have duff ends.' And he cut it in two and put half on each plate.

On one occasion grandfather had to be taken fifty miles to a Cardiff-bound French steamer. The brothers put their father safely on board, and then on their return were overtaken by what my father later described as one of the worst gales and snowstorms he had ever been in. For more than thirty hours the two boys in their 50-foot sailing cutter fought the storm and never expected to live through it. But, as my father wrote: 'We were watched over and protected by our heavenly father', and eventually they regained harbour, battered, shaken but safe.

At the end of his five years apprenticeship he became engaged to my mother, but it was then necessary for him to go to sea again for two years, in a full-rigged ship, in order to qualify as a pilot. In August 1889 he again set sail from the East Dock, Cardiff, in a full-rigged ship called the *Rajore*. I quote again from his 'Reminiscences':

'We anchored in Barry Roads for the night, and in the morning we were towed to about ten miles outside Lundy Island, and then set sail. The wages for an Able Bodied Seaman sailing from Cardiff were £3 a month, but the Liverpool owners would not pay that amount, but as the rate of pay for an A.B. was £2.10s a month, at Liverpool, they signed on the men there and sent them round to Cardiff in a Liverpool tug boat, and they joined the ship in Cardiff Roadstead, Cardiff riggers having taken us from the East Dock to the Roads. I have often wondered how women lived at home on their half pay—£1. 5s a

The Rajore, c. 1890.

month—left by the men. It did not matter so much to me, as I was unmarried then, and no one depended on me. I think it would have done some shipowners good to be sent on what turned out to be a two years' voyage.

'Some of the sailors had very little clothing, because they had spent their last voyage's money in "riotous living". One middle-aged man named Walker, had been paid off with £60 only a fortnight before, and was in a sorry plight, especially after coming round in a tug-boat from Liverpool . . .

'After we had been at sea about four weeks, the Captain while walking the poop deck suddenly turned to me as I was steering the ship and said, "Jones, when I was in Cardiff I heard you were a local preacher." "No, sir," said I, "I cannot preach." He replied, "I have heard different, so you must preach to the men on Wednesday next." (The Captain used to hold a Church of England service on Sundays).

'At 6.30 p.m. on the following Wednesday he sent an apprentice— the usual procedure every Sunday evening wind and weather permitting—to the for'castle head to strike the bell, and 29 of the crew came to the large cabin, some out of curiosity, to hear Jones preach. Three were left on deck, the officer in charge, the man at the wheel, and the one on the look out. The Captain opened the service, and I had the joy, tremblingly, of telling those men how I was saved, and how God was waiting to save them. But what an ordeal for a young sailor . . . I was able to continue those services every evening when weather permitted and had the joy also of knowing three of the men claiming Jesus as their Saviour.

'To live with those men was a great trial of faith. I stayed up many a watch below in order to perfect myself as a sailor, learning all kinds of knots, etc., so that I might not bring reproach upon my Lord. One day I came "off my watch on deck" and found only the boards left in my bunk-bed, bed-clothes, books, including my Bible, all taken away. It appears one sailor had bet a pound of tobacco that he would make me swear, and a young man who believed in me took up the bet. I knew nothing of this, and when I saw what they had done . . . I asked "What's your little game, now?"

'I can see even now the coarse faces of those men, watching me. I went round to each bunk, and gathered my things, till I came to the last man, who pretended to be asleep, on my pillow. After asking him three times, and seeing he did not intend to give it up, I'm afraid I handled him rather roughly, and took it from him. I was the only one in the starboard watch who had a pillow, the other ten used their sailor bags. Needless to say, the young man won his pound of tobacco, and they never troubled my bunk again, least of all the man who took my pillow.'

The rough treatment that my father meted out consisted as he told us in later life, in grabbing the man by the hair, pulling him up, snatching away the pillow and banging the fellow's head down hard two or three times on the boards of the bunk.

However, even this firm retaliation did not save him from the odd joke. There was one he quite enjoyed telling us about. His usual expression of surprise was 'By Jingo'. A valued possession was a small printed text, simply bearing the words 'Saved by grace', that he used to hang above his bunk. One day he went into the for'castle to find that this had been changed, so that it now read: 'Saved, by Jingo'.

To continue, however, with his own reminiscences.

'Those were lonely days at sea; the carpenter, sail-maker, cook and steward worked throughout the day, and slept at night, whereas the remainder of the crew (Captain excepted) kept their four hour watches. I used to sleep on deck, it being far too hot to sleep in the for'castle.

'In due time we arrived at Cape Town, 62 days on the passage . . . and after a little more than a month's stay we sailed in ballast for Calcutta. We anchored till next day in Table Bay; then sailed out between the mainland and Robben Island . . . There is not much to record during that passage out; one heavy breeze blew a number of our sails clean out of their ropes. We spent a full month cleaning the holds, washing, chipping iron rust, and painting, ready for the general cargo to be shipped at Calcutta . . .

'I must pass over much—the hours spent in the for'castle, forced to listen to conversations that often cast me down, especially when they associated the name of the Lord Jesus with everything that was vile. Yet such might have been my condition but for God's grace and mercy.

'We arrived at Sands Head on December 26th, and anchored about two miles from the Eastern Lightship, launched the long boat and pulled to the pilot-boat anchored nearly three miles from us, and had orders to lay at anchor till sent for . . . After a few days the tug-boat came with our orders, and we were taken in tow, and I had my first view of the River Hoogly. When we arrived at our moorings in the river—no docks there then—I was greatly interested to see the way the coolie riggers moored us. They shackled our cables on the underneath part of the buoys under the water—how they held their breath so long I don't know.

'How glad I was to get letters from home—no one on board had so many as I had. I had also the privilege of meeting the Christians—and by their request preached the Gospel one Sunday evening. It was terribly hot and only made possible by a native in the lobby turning a large wheel which turned a huge fan in the hall.

'We were a month loading in Calcutta with general cargo, this being shipped from lighters by coolies, and to my great disappoint-memt the ship was ordered to New York, instead of England. The crew were dissatisfied in port as well as at sea with the poorness of the food. I'm glad that the Board of Trade has rectified matters consider-ably in the food line. I have seen the large tin (usually called the kid) brought in from the galley for eleven men; it was supposed to be liver, but was so disgustingly cooked and poor looking, that we put it as it was on top of the half deck for the large black birds, which were plenti-ful on that river. It was enough to make hungry men who couldn't eat the food revolt; I'm glad it was not always so, but on such occasions, I used to ask the dinghy-wallah, who lay alongside in his half covered canoe-shaped boat, to make me a little rice and curry, for which I paid him . . .

'We finished loading on Saturday, but our Captain would not sail on Sunday. Two other full-rigged ships towed down past us, one close astern of the other, but the next day they were towed back, both badly damaged, where one had rammed the other. When our Captain saw them, he said, "There, you see what they got for their Sunday sailing.'

'Walker, the sailor that I referred to earlier, who arrived on board in Cardiff Roads, who had dissipated his last voyage earnings of £60 in a fortnight, was a rough character, and in Cape Town narrowly escaped drowning by falling between the ship and quay while under the influence of drink. A very ignorant man, he was induced to attend the meetings when at sea, and I could see a desire to break loose from his life of sin. He went to a Gospel meeting in the Seamen's Institute in Calcutta, and there determined to live a different life, and said he trusted Jesus.

'When we got to sea, two of the men with whom he had formerly companied in Liverpool, made up their minds to harass and hinder him, and so effectively did they work, giving him little peace of mind and continually reminding him of his past life, that one day he came to me very downhearted and said, "Oh, Jones, I think they will soon drive me out of my mind." What was I to do? The poor fellow had no one to turn to but me; a middle aged man, he could neither read nor write and didn't seem to be able to defend himself, and I also felt that they were too much for me, but first seeking the help of the Lord, I spoke to the worst of the two men in the presence of the whole watch. I said, "When Walker was like you, a blackguard, it was 'hail fellow, well met', but now he is desirous of leading a clean life, and is not using the filthy language he formerly used, you are trying to drive him out of his mind. I stand here before you, and in God's Name I take my stand with Walker, and anyone who interferes with him, will have to take me into account."

'I expected him to call me out for a fight, especially as he was strong, lusty young man, but God held him in check, for which I was very glad. I am glad to record that Walker was not much troubled after that, and it was a joy many a time to sit down on deck and teach him such simple Scriptures as Matthew 11:28, John 5:24 etc. His ignorance was appalling, but how proud he was when he had learned some of them perfectly.

'One dark night when it was his "look out" I walked to the after part of the for'castle head and called out, "Walker, what is the best news?" To my surprise he called back, "The blood of Jesus Christ, His Son, cleanseth from all sin." This was evidence of a great change in his life.

'We arrived in New York, the passage having occupied about ten months, and all the sailors, except an ordinary seaman and myself were paid off. The last I heard of Walker was that he had bought some Gospel tracts after he had his pay and gave them to some of the men.

Old John Lane, another sailor nearly 70 years of age, also professed to trust the Saviour on the passage. Poor old man; having lived a life of sin he was a pathetic sight sitting on deck reading the Bible I loaned him and asking me to explain it. When the crew left the ship to be paid off, old John stayed on board a day longer, so as not to mix up with the other men, because he knew they would expect him to join them in the drinking saloons. The steward, who unknown to us, had practised hypocrisy, to keep in the Captain's favour, took old John ashore the next day, and John, thinking all would be well with him, went for a walk. Result: the steward induced him to have a glass for old friendship's sake, and once he had tasted it the old craving came back, and he arrived back at the ship acting like a madman. Poor fellow; the chief and second mates could do nothing with him, and called me to see what I could do, for they were genuinely sorry for him.

'I did not smoke myself, but went to the carpenter and asked him to put some tobacco in his pipe and light it, and with it in my mouth I went forward to where John was carrying on. What a sight he looked —it made me real sad. I called out, "John, I want you to come and have a smoke." He quietened, and came all trembling, took the pipe and began smoking, and allowed me to lift and carry him into the for'castle and put him in his bunk. I remained with him a while and presently the pipe slipped out of his mouth and he slept for several hours. The officers wondered how it was done, but I knew my Heavenly Father was helping me.

'The next morning John was heartbroken . . . and told me all about it. What would you have done to that steward? Here were my efforts for months, my readings with John, my prayers, all seeminly dashed to the ground in a few hours. I went aft to the steward—an elderly man —and calling him to the cabin door, I said, "You double-dyed hypocrite, it is only your age that keeps me from dragging you out on deck, and giving you the trouncing you deserve." I don't say that my attitude was Christ-like because I knew it wasn't but I felt righteously angry.

'The next day I took John, by the chief mate's orders, across Brooklyn Bridge to New York side, and saw him on board a liner for Liverpool, where he expected to go into a Seamen's Home, provided for old sailors, and then sent on £20 which fortunately he had not with him when he went ashore before. I am glad to have been of some service to him. When he shook hands with me and said goodbye, he said, "Thank you for all you've done for me." The tears ran down his weather-beaten face, as he was what is termed a "hard case", and but for the mercy of God would have been outward bound again, drugged, beaten (as I have seen them), robbed of his pay and his outfit of the smallest.

'I longed for home, and with this in view went on board a steamer bound to Cardiff, expecting to sail in a few days, my object being to work my passage home, as I could not afford to pay my passage in one of the liners. But I was too late, for the mate had shipped a man an hour before. I decided to remain by the ship, which was what the Captain and Officers advised me to do.

'I think my time in New York was one of the hardest of my experience. No crew on board save the two apprentices, an ordinary seaman, myself, and the carpenter, and some of the days the hottest that New York had experienced for 20 years, and on one of those days the chief mate ordered us to get 60 fathoms of cable out of the chain locker into the between decks and drag it along the length of the ship and stow it in the storeroom, under the cabin, to trim the ship, using of course a handy-billy tackle to haul a few links at a time. That heartless mate would not get sailors to do it today.

'We loaded our cargo of 83,000 cases of "case oil" for Calcutta. Although we had been now nearly twelve months from Cardiff, and the ship's bottom must have been foul, we did not go into dry dock in New York, the consequence being that we were 183 days on the passage to Calcutta, being overdue and reported missing . . .

'The Captain had the greatest difficulty to get a crew, so with six short we towed out to Sandy Hook and anchored. The next day a tugboat came alongside, and a treacherous-looking boarding-house keeper came on board with the men. Among them were two smart, well dressed young men who had been "shanghaied"; they had never been to sea before. One of them (as we learned later) was the sole support of his widowed mother, who had worked in an office. They had never been in the boarding house of this man, so owed him nothing, but he forced them to sign the paper for three months' advance money, about £10, and the Captain was powerless to intervene. Because one refused to sign the boarding-house keeper beat him in the cabin and forced him to sign. The result was that when we got to sea neither of them were of any use as sailors, and were reduced to £1 a month, so that after a passage of six months they were in debt to the ship £4. What a shame that such things were allowed! That poor widow would never know where her son was, until she would get news from him many months later.

'I shall always remember that long passage; shortage of food but epecially shortage of water, and how eagerly we welcomed the rain both for drinking purposes and washing our clothes. When we towed up the River Hoogly, several other ships who had heard we were lost, gave three cheers for the *Rajore*. God hears and answers prayer.

'As we were loaded with "case oil" we had to stop at a berth in the river about 16 miles from the city. I was given the job to tally out the cargo. This work occupied more than three weeks, as it was done by hand, by coolies.

'One Sunday I thought I would like to go up to the city to a service, but when I got to the small station I could not get near it because of the large number of natives there. The official, seeing me, elbowed his way through the men and brought me through. When I got into the train there were several high-caste gentlemen in my compartment. One of them told me that the large number of natives I had seen had come to the waters of the Ganges to "wash away their sins". It only occurred once every twenty years. Some had walked hundreds of miles, assured that if they could only bathe in its waters all would be well. Many died from exhaustion. Some had to be carried down the wide steps to the river to be dipped, too far gone to walk further. How I thanked God that I had been born where the true story of God's love was being told out. I felt very sad as I saw hundreds of these poor spiritually blind people bowing down to temples, in which was a god or goddess, situated on the banks of a river.

'When discharged we were towed up abreast the city, and there loaded jute, linseed oil, etc., for Dundee.

'I need not weary you with the return passage, only to record that we had to call at St Helena to get some food—biscuits, potatoes, etc. The island is steep and can be approached very closely without danger, but to my surprise the Captain "hove to" about five miles off.

We launched the long boat, and three others with myself were chosen to pull the Captain ashore. We spent three to four hours ashore, and with the boat well loaded, started to pull back to the ship. Unfortunately, the mate had kept the ship hove to on the same tack, and the ship had "head reached" some miles further out to sea. We pulled and pulled, but with so much in the boat and the sea a bit choppy we could make no headway. Presently a small sailing whaleboat about 20 feet long passed us bound back to the island, and when a bargain was struck the Captain paid him the few shillings he had left, and between pulling and towing we at last got within hail of the ship.

'The Captain, who was almost beside himself with anger, rose and shouted, "Shiver the mizzen, you lubber!" and when the mate did the ship stopped "head reaching" and we got on board, stiff and sore. Oh yes, I shall remember that pull. Prior to this the Captain had chaffed me when I was at the wheel about the Bristol Channel pilots, and how he would do his own piloting, and when later on he began the same banter, I said, "Sir, you would never take this ship up the Bristol Channel with an easterly wind if you 'bout ship' every five miles from the shore". He didn't joke with me any more about piloting in the Bristol Channel.

'We arrived safely at Dundee, August 1891, having been two years and eleven days since we left Cardiff . . .

'Next day I arrived at Cardiff. After a week's holiday I again entered the pilotage service . . . Perhaps the most important time of my life was marriage to Miss Lydia Evans, who through rough and smooth has been my most faithful companion, and who is now sitting with me busy with her needle.'

Lydia Evans, aged about twenty-one.
(Painting photographed by Adrian Goldsworthy.)

CHAPTER 3

Throughout the two years my father was away he and my mother corresponded regularly, and in addition to his many long letters he sent her picture postcards from every town he visited; by the time he arrived home she had a marvellous collection of them.

When my parents married, they moved into a small house, not far from Bute Esplanade and it was there that the older members of the family were born. There were eventually six of us, two boys and four girls: Lewis, the eldest; Lillian; Gwenneth; myself; Leonard; and Mildred, the youngest, usually known as Mick. There was quite a gap in years between the older and the younger three, so that my mother used to say that she had two separate families.

My father's full name, incidentally, was Lewis Dawkin Jones and it was at this time, finding four other families called Jones in the same street, that purely to avoid confusion, he started habitually using the Dawkin. Gradually Dawkin-Jones came to be accepted as my parents' surname and it was with this name that my brothers, sisters and I grew up.

During those years there was not much money to spare and little, if any, could be saved. In spite of this, my father would part with his last half-crown on the strength of a hard-luck story, and no Saturday night ever passed without a little package being put by each child's bedside. It might not contain much, but there was always a bag of sweets and some kind of game, toy, or drawing book and crayons, to be found on Sunday morning.

Yes, we had a lovely home life. But there was discipline. With my parents one could go so far and no further, and if one didn't behave one was brought to book.

My father was a happy man, who enjoyed his home and family and had a marvellous sense of humour. However, jokes about certain topics—the Bible, or hymns—were taboo. (Only once did I make him —rather reluctantly—laugh at a joke of this sort, when after hearing of the man in the Bible who was 'sick of the palsy' I muttered: 'I bet he was.')

Lewis, right, with his brother Harry.

He spent his working life among tough, hard-bitten men, many of them heavy drinkers and heavy swearers. Yet he never had any hesitation in speaking out strongly about his faith and about right and wrong. And the great majority of men respected him for this.

There were, of course, exceptions. One particularly unpleasant character, a hulking bully, who had no use for 'all that religion', really seemed to hate my father. One day, seeing him walking alone, he came up and started taunting him, calling him a milksop and a coward and eventually blocking his path and challenging him to a fight. Inevitably, within a few seconds, a small crowd of interested onlookers had gathered. My father was a peaceful man but on this occasion there seemed no choice but to fight. He took his coat off and began to roll up his sleeves, undoubtedly uttering a silent prayer as he did so.

At that moment another dock worker appeared on the scene. He was even more hulking than the first one—and known by my father to be far from a model citizen. He stared in amazement.

'What's going on 'ere? Lewis Jones fighting in the street? I don't believe it!'

'It's not by choice,' my father told him.

'Oh, that's the way of it, is it? Right, you step aside. *I'll* take care of this.'

And take care of 'this' he did, very efficiently and then went happily on his way.

God sometimes sends very unexpected answers to prayer.

I adored my father. He used to work irregular hours, and so his meals would have to be kept hot for him. I remember as a tiny tot I would climb up onto his lap as soon as he started to eat and—although I'd had my own supper—he would put a little pile of his food to one side of the plate, give me my own fork and let me eat with him. Greedy little creature, I'd end up having about a quarter of his dinner.

Mind you, it was awfully easy to eat too much in our house, because my mother was such a superb cook. In addition to the daily meals she did all her own baking, the day of the Big Bake being Friday.

First, there was always the rich fruit cake. Then there might be coconut tarts, delicious concoctions of coconut, sugar, egg, and jam, that vanished as soon as they were cold. Sometimes there was sweet-cake—a cake with eggs and sugar, but no fat, which was buttered and cut like bread. Often there were custard tarts, which would put modern shop ones to shame; or pastry cases, in which to put dollops of jam and cream, when cold. Another week there could be sponge cakes. Or again, golden brown scones, made with bicarbonate of soda, cream of tartre and sour milk. These were tipped while still hot onto a clean cloth, to catch the steam, so that the outsides would be soft; delicious things—one could never have enough of them. In addition, there were nearly always Welsh cakes, without which no baking day would be complete—stacks of them, on a huge dish, each one sugared as it was removed from the bakestone. There were, too, invariably, apple tarts, or other fruit pies, according to season, decorated with pastry leaves or sugared on top. Occasionally, for a change, there was apple cake. This was another version of apple tart, except that it was oblong in shape, and cooked without sugar on a bakestone. Turning it was something of an art, but when it was finally cooked it was a rich dark brown. The top was then carefully taken off, fine sugar and nutmeg added, and the top replaced. It was then cut into squares and eaten hot or cold.

Last but not least there was bread: gorgeous golden loaves with delicious crusts which one never gets on shop bread. The dough was put to rise over the cooker in the most enormous enamel bowl, covered with a clean linen cloth. Later it was cut up and kneaded and transferred to four oblong tins, after which a lovely aroma permeated the house. Some weeks there were currant loaves, which one could eat and eat and never want to stop.

Apart from the Big Bake there was each day to cater for, and everything was home-made. There was always a roast on Sundays, usually cold meat and fried potatoes on Mondays—that was washing day. Other days we would have enormous steak and kidney pies, or stuffed hearts with mint sauce, roast breasts of lamb with parsley stuffing, beef stews, home-made faggots, etc. A stockpot was always kept going, started off in the first instance with rich marrow bones. Then was added pearl barley and vegetables—onions, carrots, celery, turnips—and it was boiled indefinitely. There was a ladle at hand, and anyone who wanted soup just helped themselves.

My mother made my sisters and me all learn to cook while we were very young. 'I know you're all going to get married,' she would say, 'and you're not going to be foisted on to some poor man and be unable to cook him a meal.' As a result, before I left school I could cook a full dinner with the best.

I well remember, though, the first meal I insisted on cooking, entirely on my own, for the whole family. I think I was about sixteen. It was to be a full three-course dinner—soup, a roast and two vegetables, and a pudding. The actual cooking went quite smoothly, but I had had no experience in getting everything dished up and onto the dining room table, on time and unaided. When I took the soup in, I still had to make the gravy and get the vegetables into their dishes.

'Please start without me,' I said, after I'd deposited the soup tureen on the table, and I dashed back to the kitchen.

I managed to get the whole of the main course into the dining room by the time soup was being finished. However, the pudding—of which I had high hopes—was still being cooked and I hadn't made the sauce. Again, I told them to carry on and scooted out to the kitchen once more. I took the pudding off, made the sauce, which took rather longer than anticipated—and hurried with my *pièce de rèsistance* back into the dining room to find the others just finishing off the main course.

At last I was able to sit down, and I waited anxiously for the reactions. The pudding was approved. The whole meal was approved. I sat back, basking in the general congratulations and enjoying my own helping of pudding. Yes, it was really very good.

Something, however, seemed wrong. I could not think what it was. It wasn't until I'd finished the helping that I realized I still felt rather hungry. Then I gave a gasp of annoyance.

'I haven't had my proper dinner!' I said indignantly. 'I started with the pudding. What a swiz!'

Needless to say I received no sympathy for my deprivation—only ribald laughter from all sides.

However, I wasn't to be beaten. I'd cooked the meal and I was going to sample it all. So I next had a plate of roast meat, potatoes and greens, now somewhat tepid, and ended up, defiantly, with a positively cold dish of soup.

I do not honestly recommend dinners eaten backwards.

My parents gave all of us children private secondary education—

and quite a struggle it must have been. But we all started out at the local Board School, as it was then called. And I have never regretted this. When I hear these days of teachers being afraid to go to school, because of what the pupils might do to them; of children disobeying orders, using violence and obscene language; of teachers going on strike, it utterly amazes me. It all seems completely alien to the idea of school as I knew it.

I can close my eyes now and be instantly back in my Board School. What a lovely school it was! The building itself seemed wonderfully solid—the thick grey stone walls, the dark wood desks, the heavy doors.

Every day was started with Prayers, plus a hymn and the recitation of a verse or two of Scripture. Then it was straight down to lessons. And a marvellous education we were given. A thorough grounding in the three Rs was the first essential. In arithmetic we had to repeat all our tables, from two to twelve every day. Any time in my life since I can give the answer to any multiplicaton problem instantly without having to work it out—as indeed most of us could. Because the tables were drummed into us.

Eleanor St. School, Cardiff.

45

Reading included reading aloud, with proper diction and pronunciation insisted upon. These days it does not seem to be thought important for children—or even teachers—to learn decent speech. It seems highly peculiar to me that so many teachers are unable to speak good English. Even if they were never taught to do so, you'd think they would want to teach themselves.

Once a week we would have a spelling bee. Boys would line up one side of the room and girls the other. Then a word would be called out to the first in each line and if he or she failed to get it right would have to sit down. It was rather like musical chairs. Eventually only one from each side would be left standing. And the girl was invariably me. I realize now that spelling was the only thing I was really good at.

However, all this was only the basic part of our education. We were also taught history, geography, botany, science, drawing and singing (using the tonic-sol-fa method). There was sewing and cooking for the girls, carpentry for the boys. (No doubt today this would be considered sexist.) Every day when the weather was fine there was 'drill' in the playground—needless to say we had no gym. There was even the opportunity to do Welsh, but I found myself utterly unable to cope with it and after a while was excused it—something I have ever since regretted.

Our favourite day of the school year was Empire Day. After prayers we would all troop to the main hall for recitations from poems extolling the Empire and for patriotic songs—ending up always with 'Flag of Britain, Proudly Waving'. How all this would be frowned on today! Afterwards—this probably the main appeal of the occasion—we would be given the rest of the day off.

Empire Day, though, was an exception. Most of the time everyone worked extremely hard. The teachers were really dedicated people, who seemed genuinely to want us to learn. We stood in awe of them but respected them. They were kind but would stand no nonsense. In all the years I was there I never heard the toughest boy—or girl—answer back or misbehave in any way during school hours. Nor, although some of the children came from very poor homes, do I ever remember any swearing.

I cannot say I truly enjoyed school, but I learnt things there that have benefited me all my life and I am very grateful for it.

I was certainly happier, too, at my Board school than at the private school my parents sent me to when I was eleven—even though I found myself academically quite up to and even above the standard of girls who had been at private school since they were five.

After my grandfather Evans died, Grandmother went to live with her daughter Miriam, now married and living in another part of Cardiff, and my parents moved to 4 Bute Esplanade. Here they were very happy. However, some years later we moved to a house (No. 6) in Windsor Esplanade, just a stone's throw away. I think I was about six years old at the time. I had been home from school with a cold and my main recollection of the event is holding my father's hand as we walked to the new house, and my only emotion being fear in case somebody saw me and reported to the teacher that I was out of doors and not ill at all.

Number Six was slightly larger than our old home; it was of three storeys, with two 'reception rooms' as the estate agents call them, a

Windsor Esplanade.

47

large yet cosy kitchen with a black-leaded grate, and a scullery; four bedrooms (the main one with a balcony) and a bathroom on the first floor; and two attic bedrooms. It faced south and got a lot of sun.

It was, moreover, right on the sea front and had a fine view of the Bristol Channel. My father could now do his studying in his own very large front bedroom, with his telescope, or 'spyglass' as he called it, to hand and keep an eye on all the shipping traffic in the Channel. He always took a great interest in everything that went on and in those days there was a constant flow of shipping—mostly merchantmen, but also the occasional 'man o' war', as well as many smaller craft, such as the pleasure boats that throughout the summer months sailed every day to places along the Devon and Somerset coast: Lynton, Lynmouth, Ilfracombe, Clevedon, Weston-Super-Mare. When we went on these cruises ourselves we always used to run to the rail as the steamer left Cardiff for the reverse view—Windsor Esplanade from the sea. It stood out most elegantly, with only the Wall, less than twenty yards from our front door, keeping the sea at bay . . .

(The following description of the Wall is adapted from an article my son wrote for *The Times* some years ago and is reproduced by permission.)

I give the Wall a captial letter because it was so obviously a personality in its own right. It was a superb structure: made of grey granite bricks, it was 4 feet high, with a flat, smooth top about a foot wide. The near side was vertical, but the far side sloped, so that the Wall widened to about three feet at the bottom. It ran the entire length of the Esplanade, curving at right angles at the far western end, to continue in front of the adjoining road, Penarth Terrace. All in all it was nearly three hundred yards long.

Beyond the Wall there was a stretch of stones, of odd shapes and rather unevenly set, running down at a slight angle for about twenty feet. Then, at low tide, mud flats, dotted here and there with patches of coarse grass. At high tide the mud would be under water; and then the sea would normally just reach the row of stones. At spring tides, however, it would reach the Wall, and sometimes even come two or three feet up it. In really rough weather the waves would send spray dashing over on to the pavement. At such times we children loved playing a sort of acquatic 'last across'—scrambling up till our eyes just topped the Wall, watching for the biggest waves coming, then dropping down and dashing away at the last second to avoid a soaking. Needless to say, it was a game usually nipped in the bud by grown-ups just when it was starting to get interesting.

Only once in all the years I lived there did the Wall let us down. There was an excepionally high tide and the Esplanade was covered about eight or nine inches deep with sea water. I do not think any got into the houses, but I still remember the excitement of paddling in the front garden.

After high tides there were nearly always interesting things to be found on the stones over the Wall: there would be balls, washed from the seaside resorts along the coast—much more fun to play with than those bought by our parents. Sometimes great tree trunks would arrive, when the Esplanaders, like medieval villagers dividing the spoils of the hunt, would turn out with saws and choppers for valuable supplies of firewood. On occasions, after heavy weather, fishing smacks or yachts, that had been torn from their moorings farther along the coast, would be swept aground on to our stones. Once an actual tug was swept off course and finished up high and dry only a hundred yards out.

Less pleasant things were sometimes deposited—the rotting body of some dog, cat or even sheep. A message would then be sent to the sanitary inspector's office and men would come and remove the offending corpse. We children would be instructed not to play over the Wall until the sea had given the stones a thorough washing.

The tide, though, would take things, as well as leave them. Over the Wall was an extremely useful place to dispose of garden refuse. With careful timing, hedge and lawn clippings, weeds and so on could be thrown over shortly before high tide and would be borne away on the crest of a wave.

During periods when the sea covered it for a time every day the mud would be dark and soft and slippery. But it was quite safe and one could never sink more than a few inches into it. A favourite sport of many of the boys—and some girls—from the back street houses at these times was mud-larking—just taking off nearly all their clothes and sliding about in it until they were quite indistinguishable from blacks. They could usually find some gully with a foot or so of water in it in which to wash the mud—or most of it—off afterwards. But it was terribly clinging stuff and I'm sure there were many muddy areas left under their clothes when they went home. This game was absolutely forbidden to us and I must say I did not feel particularly deprived by the prohibition.

We concentrated on searching for crabs, shrimps and small fish in the little pools that would be left behind. Or we would cook meals on the stones—sausages or potatoes baked in their jackets on a wood fire. Over the Wall was a lovely place for this sort of thing; you were near enough to home to fetch things you'd forgotten, yet the great bulk of the Wall gave a sense of privacy and remoteness.

During the summer months when a period of low tides coincided with hot and dry weather the mud would harden to form a fine, huge 'field' for all sorts of games—cricket and out-of-season football for the boys, hockey for the girls, rounders for everyone. The pitch tended to break up rather quickly, but there was so much space one just moved fifty yards on. In later years this tendency of the mud to break up was turned to good use when there was a craze for dirt-track racing on bikes.

In the summer days, too, the Esplanade was a popular place for the office girls from Mountstuart Square to have their lunch and many of them would bring their sandwiches to eat sitting on our wall. We children graciously decided to permit this.

At weekends, also, we were quite a little tourist centre, with many people coming to enjoy the fine channel view: Queen's Dock to the left, Penarth Head to the right, with St Augustine's Church standing out, and, as it were framed between, the Flat and Steep Holms, seeming by a trick of perspective to be practically adjoining. (I well remember my surprise when I first went on a cruise to discover how far apart they actually were.) On clear days the Somerset coast, with Brean Down and the Mendip Hills behind could be seen. I sometimes think now that a sweet and ice cream stall in our front garden would have been a profitable venture, but perhaps on the other hand competition would soon have become razor keen, with a stall outside every house.

In fact, for most of the time the Esplanade was a very quiet place.

The View from Windsor Esplanade.

The Wall was our own, to lean against or sit on. As a small child, of course, one had to be lifted up to see over the top, but one generally grew big enough laboriously to scramble up oneself. Everybody had his or her favourite footholds. But the more agile young people scorned this and did a sort of two handed vault, combined with a hundred and eighty degree twist in the air, which left them sitting on the Wall, looking back at the houses; then a quick raising of the legs and a spin round, and they would be immediately facing out to sea. It was a proud day in my life when after years of vain attempts and scraped knees I first achieved this feat.

However, this was a long way in the future when we first moved to Number Six.

CHAPTER 4

I still feel that that part of Cardiff was a rather special place. Within a minute's walk of Number Six lived people of every class, from dock labourers, through tradesmen, to well-to-do professional people. Yet there seemed to be little class feeling—certainly none whatsoever among the children. Moreover, we were surrounded by people who for one reason or another one could never forget for as long as one lived. Take first, for example, the tradesmen and shopkeepers with whom we dealt. Outstanding among these were old Mrs Pickford and her daughter, Clara. They kept a tiny shop which, I must admit, we never patronised unless we had to. They seemed never to close. Yet on the other hand, they were never fully open, for one of the double doors was always locked. This made the entrance extremely narrow, so you had to squeeze through sideways. It was as if they wanted to make things as difficult for their customers as possible.

As you entered, an enormous bell over the door clanged like a churchbell—and then the smell hit you. A smell of paraffin, and kippers, and vinegar from a great cask, and fresh paint (they were constantly having the shop repainted in bright green). I can close my eyes today and smell that shop. It was always crowded—partly because it was so small, and partly because Mrs and Miss Pickford seemed to sell practically anything anyone could want.

The shop was full to the door—with firewood (or sticks, as they were called), all done up in neat bundles, fire-lighters, potatoes, cabbages and onions. All the groceries were piled up on open shelves —no glass cases or even cupboards. Mrs Pickford and Clara were both spotlessly clean, wore long pinafores, and curling pins all over their heads, which they apparently never took out. They had tight mouths. Mrs Pickford's head shook slightly all the while. Clara—prim and proper and plump—was obviously the head of the house. Their voices were thin and petulant-sounding and they used them as little as possible—never said 'good morning' or 'call again' and certainly never smiled. They just served non-stop in complete silence. They seemed to resent your going in there at all. As you entered they looked at you as if to say: 'Oh no, not another one!' You then had to be prepared to stand quietly—never daring to talk to the other customers —until they were ready to serve you. It was like the two minutes' silence at a Remembrance Day service.

One day, to our utter astonishment, we heard that Clara had got married. 'Married?' we said. 'It's impossible! Nobody'd marry Clara.'

But it was true; and in the course of time Clara had a baby. 'I'd love to see it,' I said. 'I bet it's been born with curling pins in its hair.'

I will say one thing, though, for Mrs Pickford's: I'll never forget it. People in fifty years will never be able to look back with nostalgia at today's supermarkets.

Nearly opposite Pickford's was the grocers, Dakin's. This was as dirty a shop as Pickford's was clean. Although every day Mr Dakin would put sawdust on the floor, he would lay it on top of the previous day's layer, so that after an hour the old sawdust would be showing through all over the place.

Regularly each Saturday night Mr Dakin would get drunk. He would go to the pub on his bicycle. At the close of the evening he would usually start off trying to ride it home, though would usually end up pushing it. On arrival he would take the bicycle indoors and somehow struggle with it to the top of the stairs. Then he would let it fall to the bottom. This, you could say, was his Saturday treat.

Mrs Dakin, perhaps not surprisingly, was an unsmiling woman, who looked as though she had been at the bottom of the stairs every time he'd done it.

Dakin's was another shop we never used if we could avoid it. We went to a shop called 'Beatty's'. Opposite Beatty's was Mr Farrant's bakery. Mr Farrant was a lovely old man—very tall and thin, with a long black beard, which I'm sure must often have dangled in the dough. My younger brother, Len, was a particular friend of his and we all used to go and watch Mr Farrant at work.

I remember the long scrubbed wooden bench down one side of the bakery; the enormous oven at the far end, which seemed to us to go back for miles when Mr Farrant pushed the loaves in; the long, long pole with the flat shovel at the end, with which he used to get them out. I remember the long thin rolls, called 'busters', that he used to give us.

And did Mr Farrant make the most gorgeous bread? Well, frankly, no. It was very heavy and quite horrible. As I said, my mother used to do her own baking and this perhaps spoiled us for shop bread. Maybe today Mr Farrant's bread would seem superb.

Years later, when Mr Farrant retired, the premises were taken over by an old and filthy man, who opened it as a potato shop. At least, that is apparently all he sold. One could just see a big barrel of them inside the door. It was impossible to see any more, because the shop was always in almost total darkness. To go inside, even if one had wished to, was virtually impossible, because of the large and ferocious looking Alsation dog, which sat continuously outside the door and growled menacingly at everyone who approached. The owner had no known name, was referred to by everybody simply as 'the old man', and I never saw a single customer go into the shop. Could it have been merely a front for some criminal organisation, I wonder? I'd almost like to think so.

It is strange how some houses seem to attract dramatic events. Next door to us lived a succession of neighbours, all of whom were involved in tragedies or bizarre occurrences. The first ones I recollect were a Captain and Mrs Hawkins. They were a charming couple, with a little girl, and I remember they always addressed each other as 'Mummy' and 'Daddy', even when the child wasn't present. One week the Captain's sister came to stay, and on the Friday morning we suddenly heard loud shrieks from next door. My mother and her brother Yant, who happened to be present, rushed in and found a hysterical Mrs Hawkins sobbing: 'I knew they shouldn't have let her out.' They discovered that her sister-in-law had drowned herself in the bath. It transpired that she had only just been released from a mental home.

The Hawkins' were succeeded by a wealthy pork butcher called Brewer and his wife. They were a rather unpleasant couple, who never spoke to us. One night my parents were woken by a frantic hammering on the wall. They hurried next door and found Mrs Brewer in the throes of having a baby. My father went for the doctor, but by the time he arrived, my mother had safely delivered the child.

Even after this, however, the Brewers still didn't speak to us. Some months later there was another commotion in the middle of the night —a sudden outbreak of shouting and banging. It was the police. They had come to arrest Brewer. It turned out he was the head of a smuggling gang.

Mrs Brewer moved hurriedly away, and the next occupants were a family by the name of Crawley—husband and wife, and a beautiful and exotic-looking teenage daughter called Olga. She had long raven-black hair, dark flashing eyes, and many boy friends. Every day we would see her about, cheerful, friendly and apparently perfectly normal in every way. But then in the night we'd hear her crying. She would go on, sobbing and wailing loudly in her room, for hour after hour. Then the next day she would be out and about again, seemingly as happy as a lark. It was really rather eerie, but we never were able to find out the reason for it.

The Crawleys again moved away very suddenly, and were replaced by a stockbroker, called Phillips with his wife and son, Harold— whom they always referred to as 'Hell'. Mr Phillips was a smiling, charming, gentlemanly man, looking rather like Ray Milland. Mrs Phillips was a sad little woman—and an alcoholic. Every so often Mrs Phillips would go away for a 'cure'. And each time she did so, Mr Phillips would have his lady friend to stay. We would always know when Mrs Phillips was due home, for, a day or two beforehand, a crate of whisky or gin would be delivered. After his wife had returned, Mr Phillips would go off to his office in the mornings, leaving her in a house full of liquor. In due time Mrs Phillips drank herself to death, and a few months later Mr Phillips, smiling as ever, married his lady friend and moved away.

For a short time a pilot colleague of my father, named Hall, lived next door, with his grown-up son, Leslie. Then Leslie died of tuberculosis. Finally, a Mr Short and his wife moved in, and all I can say of Mr Short is that he didn't get himself arrested, or drown himself, or drink himself to death. Unfortunately.

There were so many other neighbours of whom I have just the briefest but nevertheless vivid recollections. Mrs Bourne, a solicitor's wife, our neighbour on the other side, who, if a ball went into her garden, used to cut it in half and throw the halves back. (Len and a friend of his once nearly drove her to apoplexy, by climbing out of the attic window onto the verandah, creeping along and dangling the two halves of one of her victims on a string outside her bedroom.)

There was mad Doctor Miller, who would perform minor operations, without anaesthetics, in his surgery, and who used to play with his little boy by dangling him upside down by his ankles. Dr Miller's daughter later qualified as a doctor (though I doubt, after that treatment, if his son ever did), and was knifed in her surgery by an Arab seaman. There was Mr Hansen, as bald as a coot, who bought himself a black wig, looking just like a sweep's brush, and which used regularly to blow off and come bowling down the Esplanade, with Mr Hansen in pursuit.

And there was ghastly Mrs Rolt, a big woman, with thick ankles, a thin cowed husband, two daughters and a hateful, bad-tempered chow terrier. One of Mrs Rolt's favourite tricks was to order goods from a store C.O.D., then, when they came, pretend to pass the money to the vanman with one hand, hold out her other hand for the receipt, and as soon as she had it, snatch back the money and slam the door.

It was Mrs Rolt who poisoned my lovely old mongrel, Chum, after he'd fought with her chow. He died in my arms after careering round the room in agony for ten minutes, banging his head against the wall. We learnt later that at her previous address Mrs Rolt was known to have poisoned at least four dogs which had annoyed her precious chow.

However, Mrs Rolt had her own problems. One of her daughters went totally bald, and the baby of the other was savaged in its pram and permanently scarred by *her* dog.

Far be it from me to give the impression that every occupant of the Esplanade was a thoroughly unpleasant person. There were the Sparkes, owners of a haulage business, whose horses were the best-kept in Cardiff. They regularly took all the prizes at the annual show, after which they would be paraded through the streets of the Docks, hooves polished, manes and tails plaited, bedecked in their rosettes and medals. My sister Mick later married one of the sons of the family. There was Mr Ames, a magistrate, and his invalid wife, a childless, middle-aged couple, who took on a fifteen-year old girl,

Lizzie Roberts, from the orphanage, as maid. Lizzie looked after them dutifully for many years, and when they eventually died, she found that they had left her everything—including the house. There was the Baptist minister, another white-bearded gentleman; a succession of vicars of the nearby St Stephen's Church; our friends, the Morgans; the Stonemans, the Pattersons and many others.

There were also Mr and Mrs Lipscombe. He was a quiet, gentlemanly man and she a cheerful, bustling little woman, the daughter of a Scottish doctor. She always wore what looked exactly like a white lace doily on her head, held in place by a black bow. When I once plucked up courage to ask her why, she replied with a vague smile 'Because of the angels, dear.' I still do not know what she meant. She was apparently quoting from 1 Corinthians, chapter 11, but as this passage is concerned with women 'praying or prophesying' it hardly seemed relevant. A favourite expression of hers, when leaving you, was 'See you on a cloud, dear.'

The Lipscombes kept a small shop, selling religious books, texts, calendars, and so on, and I've known few people so utterly devoted to 'the Lord's work'. Their main interest was in mission work among foreign seamen and one of the highlights of the week for us children when we were little was the Sunday service the Lipscombes held for them in their house. We would hang about outside, waiting to see the men arrive. Every week about twenty would turn up. They would be of every nationality: blacks, Chinese, Greeks, Swedes, Poles and many others. There would always be some Arabs, usually of the type (known to the children for some reason as Agra-Johns) who wore their shirt tails outside their trousers. Heaven knows how the Lipscombes persuaded them all to come. But come they did and would crowd into the drawing-room. Then Mr or Mrs Lipscombe would preach to them. What we outside really looked forward to, though, were the hymns. Mrs Lipscombe would play the piano and lead the singing in her high soprano, and the sailors would join in—in every key available and most of them in their own tongue. How they knew what they were singing about I'll never know. I can only assume the Lipscombes had hymn books printed in every possible language. The noise was indescribable.

Whether the seamen expected some sort of refreshment before they left I'm not sure, but they didn't get it. What each got was a present: a card, a couple of inches square, bearing an illuminated text. They would troop out, all holding these little pieces of cardboard, gazing at them in a puzzled manner. Then they would stand around, muttering quietly to each other, before slowly dispersing. We would go back indoors. The entertainment was over for another week.

I must not pass from the subject of neighbours without mentioning both the Landons and the Jacksons. Neither family lived in the Esplanade, but in one of the side streets to the rear.

The Landons were one of the poor families that my mother 'adopted', making herself responsible for their welfare. (There were many such over the years.) The Landons had five children, all cross-eyed, whom their mother used to put to sleep sideways, as it were—from the head to the foot of one big bed.

One of the girls had been born on Christmas day and had consequently been christened Olivia Christmas Landon. A few years later Mrs Landon gave birth to another daughter, this time on Shrove Tuesday. Her parents had decided in advance on the first name Annie, and now there was no doubt in their mind as to what the baby's middle name was to be. It was entered on her birth certificate and she bore it proudly all her life: Annie Pancake Landon.

Near to the Landon's house, a few years later, lived the Jacksons. Mr Jackson was the local chimney sweep. With big grates in every room, and coal fires in most of them for two thirds of the year (and no smokeless fuel in those days), our chimneys, like most people's, needed regular sweeping; so Mr Jackson was a frequent visitor. He was a tiny, dirty, but very happy man. His wife was a large, buxom, grim-faced woman, who was always spotlessly clean and immaculate with white linen and stiffly ironed pinafores. How she managed it, married to the dirty little sweep, as we called him, I don't know. Side by side, Mr and Mrs Jackson looked like something out of a seaside postcard. However, against all the odds they seemed very happy, and Mr Jackson was obviously devoted to his large, taciturn wife.

Mr Jackson used to make an awful mess when working, but then all sweeps did, and he was at least cheerful with it, so we never thought of hiring anybody else. It was always, though, necessary for one of us to be present to supervise him and ensure that he took all precautions to keep the dirt down to a minimum, and one day when I was grown up it fell to me to be the supervisor.

Making conversation, I asked after his wife.

'Oh, she's OK,' he said. 'She's away. In Slough. Her sister's ill and she's keeping house for her till she's better.'

'I see. You must be missing her.'

'Aye, I am that. I went to see her last Saturday, though.'

'That's nice.' I wasn't very interested, but wished to be polite. 'So it could be worse,' I said. 'I imagine the train service to Slough is pretty good.'

'Oh, I didn't go by train,' he said. 'Couldn't afford it both ways. I went on me bike.'

I stared. For a moment I thought he was joking. But, though cheery by nature, I don't think Mr Jackson had ever made a joke in his life.

I said incredulously: 'You cycled? *To Slough?*'

'That's right.'

'But—but it's *miles*!'

''Bout hundred and forty, I reckon.'

I looked at Mr Jackson. I thought of his bicycle—a well known sight in the district: old, large-framed, heavy, and without even a three-speed gear. I thought of the road—from Cardiff, to Newport, to Chepstow, to Gloucester, to Cheltenham, to Witney, to Maidenhead. We'd done it a few times by car—it was a main route to London. And that had been tiring enough!

'You did it in a day?' I asked weakly.

'Aye. Started out at five in the morning. Took some sandwiches and a bottle of orange squash, but I didn't stop much. I just kept plugging away. I was all right.'

'How long did it take you, for heaven's sake?'

'Got there about ten at night.'

'That's incredible,' I said. 'Did Mrs Jackson know you were coming?'

'No.'

'She must have been absolutely amazed.'

He considered for a moment. 'No, not really.'

'But what did she say?'

'She opened the door and said, "What are you doing here?" "Come to see you," I told her. There she seed the bike. "You didn't come on *that*?" she said. "Yes," I said.'

Mr Jackson straightened up.

By now I was fascinated. 'Well, what did she say then?'

'She said, "You silly little b-----",' Mr Jackson told me proudly.

CHAPTER 5

It seems strange, looking back, to think that even quite ordinarily-placed families like ours were never without a servant or two in those days. When I was a girl we always had a maid, and quite memorable characters some of them were.

The first I recall was Ada Lloyd—tall, thin, rather grim, but kind. Ada considered herself very religious. She said her prayers every night. She would kneel by her bed, clasp her hands and solemnly intone: 'Thou wilt show me the path of life. Amen.' Then, her religious duty completed, she'd go to bed.

There was the very correct and superior Gladys, who every morning before she started work would gaze sadly round at the dust which had landed since her previous day's toil, sigh and say:

'Labour in vain, as it were, so to speak.'

Gladys married a man whom she never referred to as anything but 'Mine'. 'Mine was saying only yesterday . . .' 'Mine and I went to town on Saturday afternoon.'

'Mine' worked at the local dry dock and one day fell in. Dropping about forty feet onto concrete he could easily have been killed, but miraculously he landed on his feet. Apart from always being rather flat-footed after that, he made a full recovery, except that he was about four inches shorter.

Years later, Gladys and Mine's daughter, Rosie, came to work for us. Rosie seemed to do everything at a terrific pace. You'd see her flitting about the house, running up and down stairs, apparently never stopping. The strange thing was that very little work ever seemed to get done. I suppose that is a sort of gift she had. Rosie was also an all-time champion at breaking things. But she cleverly gave the impression of never actually having dropped them herself. Endowing them with a kind of independent will of their own, she would several times a week appear in the doorway with the pieces of some broken jug or bowl in her hand. 'Please, mum,' she'd say, quite unabashed, 'this fell in the sink and broke.'

I remember also Kate. Kate came to us from an orphanage at the age of fourteen. She had known nothing of family life and was blissfully happy with us. Len was a baby at the time she arrived, and Kate was crazy about him. She virtually adopted him, carrying him around with her and spending all her spare time playing with him and taking him for walks.

Kate stayed with us for six years, almost becoming one of the family. Then tragedy struck—the seemingly inevitable scourge of those days, tuberculosis. She was removed to a sanatorium in North Wales, but the doctor told my mother privately that there was little hope.

Kate had no relatives, and if it had not been for my mother would have died completely alone. Every other Sunday mother went to see the girl, always taking a little parcel of cakes, sweets, fruit or some other small present. Even today, it is a long trip, by rail, from Cardiff to North Wales. It was then at least a four-hour journey. There was no direct line and you had to change twice. Yet I do not think my mother missed one of her scheduled trips in the months until poor Kate died.

All the rest of our servants, however, pale into insignificance by comparison with our 'daily', Lena. Lena was, I think, the most unforgettable character I ever met—which is saying something. She was a person one could never meet more than once in a lifetime—or indeed would want to. She came to us first to give additional help with the laundering and scrubbing, and stayed for nearly twenty years.

Lena was tall, angular and flat—as if, somebody once said, she'd been ironed. Her face was quite hideous—long, thin and rather like a horse. She had small eyes, big, yellow teeth and coarse skin. Her hair was piled on top of her head in a round bun. In the summer she would perch on top of that a straw hat, with a hatpin through it, and in winter a brown hood, which in some way made the horselike appearance even greater. She always wore the same black dress to her ankles and over that a long black coat. I think she was perpetually in mourning for her mother, who had died about ten years before Lena came to us. On her feet were heavy lace-up boots, with the laces wound round her ankles. For work, Lena would remove her coat and don two long black aprons, and over those tie a large piece of sacking.

Lena was very simple—yet with this went a craftiness that always took care of number one. She'd had to make her own way throughout life and I don't believe had ever experienced love. I doubt she would have know what to do with it if she'd had it.

I do not believe anyone could have put in more working hours than Lena. She had a bed-sitting room in the house of her married sister and crippled 'bruvver-in-law'—as she always called him—and at about seven in the morning she set out from there to walk the two miles to Mountstuart Square, where she would clean offices for two hours. Then she'd come on to our house, arriving at about quarter to ten. Here she would do—well, really, whatever she liked. Firstly she'd prepare and eat a jolly good breakfast. She would make toast, fry bacon and eggs, get out the sauces, butter and marmalade, and brew a big pot of tea.

After a leisurely breakfast, she would commence work. She'd carry on until four or half past, get herself a very nice tea and then go back to Mountstuart Square, by the time the offices closed, and put in another two hours there. And all the time Lena worked she talked—if there was nobody present, to herself. She always had some long (and in her opinion, at least) highly dramatic story to tell. But she didn't just tell it to one person. She told it to everybody who came near her.

Nobody could escape Lena's stories—except, that is, my youngest sister, Mildred. Lena loved Mildred—or 'Melial' as she always called her (because, as she said, 'I can't say "Mildred", you see'). Miss 'Melial' could get away with anything in dealing with Lena. If anybody else had said half the things to her that Mildred said, Lena would have put her hat and coat on and vanished for good. However, as soon as she started telling her a story, Mildred would just point to the door.

'Out,' she'd say. 'At once. I don't wish to know. I can't stand looking at you today. Go. Now.'

At which Lena would double up in helpless laughter. Because Melial said it, it was hilarious. She never realized that my sister was quite serious.

Many of Lena's stories involved her own sister. She and Lena seemed always to be quarrelling. In Lena's own words: 'Me and me sister gets on better when we're not together.' Often the quarrels would seem to involve the whole family. 'So,' Lena would tell us, 'then my bruvver-in-law, wot's got no legs, he stepped in.'

Her nephew, though, would often seem to take Lena's side. 'Me nephew's very fond of me,' she would say. 'He's awful infection.'

My father, the most patient of men, who loved practically everybody in the world, could not stand Lena. She would burst in on him with mops and brooms, while he was studying and insist on starting to clean around him, even if the room didn't need it and she was supposed to be doing something else. He would come down and put on his hat and coat. 'I'm going out until that woman's gone,' he would say, and disappear for an hour or so.

At her best, in a working mood, Lena was really something, getting through an enormous amount of chores in no time. Nor do I ever remember her failing to turn up, whatever the weather. On the other hand, if she wasn't in such a mood, she might just as well not have come. You wouldn't know afterwards that she had been at all. If asked to do something she disliked, she would adopt a blank expression, as though she were miles away and just could not hear you: and nine times out of ten she'd get out of doing it. She would be constantly making excuses to go to the shops. She'd find herself mysteriously out of, say, 'Panshine', the pot cleaner we used.

'Please, mum, I'm out of Shampine,' she'd say.

'It's called Panshine, Lena,' someone would tell her.

'I know, but I can't say "Panshine", see.'

She'd take a long, long time at the shops and always come back with some new and thrilling saga.

Once a week Lena would go to the music hall. 'I went to the Empire last night,' she would confide, and then, lowering her voice: 'I went in by the side door, so the vicar wouldn't see if he went past.'

Lena was a regular churchgoer, who never missed early Communion on a Sunday, but I'm sure she only went because she thought the vicar wanted her there, and did not really have any understanding of what it was all about. I did, though, ask her once if she had a favourite hymn. 'Oh yes,' she said, 'I loves "The Church's Fun Woundation" —that's my favourite.'

On Sunday afternoon would come Lena's big treat of the week: a visit to the cemetery to see her mother's grave. 'I fell down flat on it,' she'd announce proudly the next day.

She never tired of telling us of her mother's dying words: 'Lena, I've been a good muvver to you. I've been a better muvver to you than ever your farver was.'

For many years we never knew how old Lena was. It was quite impossible to tell. Then one day we found out. She was unusually silent and long-faced. Eventually somebody asked her what the trouble was. 'Me nephew found me birf certificate last night,' she said gloomily. 'I fought I was twenty-eight, but I find I'm forty-two.'

Lena's one ambition in life was to buy herself a burial plot, so that she would not have to be buried by the Council. One day she was very excited. She'd at last saved up enough, and given the money to her nephew, who had arranged it all for her. Poor Lena. From what I had heard of that nephew, I'm sure the money went on a horse. But as she never knew, she was perfectly happy.

CHAPTER 6

They say that only the busiest people find time to help others, and this was certainly true of my mother. It would take more than one book to tell about the things she did. Yet she was never, I think, looked upon as a do-gooder—perhaps because mostly she did the good in an unobtrusive way.

There was for instance the teenage girl living near us, housekeeping for her two elder brothers. She contracted TB and was soon confined to bed. Her brothers were a pair of gentle giants, who adored their sister, but they both had to go to work. Every day, for many months, until the girl's inevitable death, my mother took her light, dainty lunches on a tray and coaxed her into eating them. She also took her little presents—linen handkerchiefs, tiny bottles of scent and the like. Her brothers used almost to cry with gratitude; but no one except them and us ever knew about it.

Again, there was the old retired sailor, who rented a single room in one of the back streets. On fine days he would sit outside on an old chair, smoking his pipe and reading the paper. My mother used regularly to stop and pass the time of day with him. Then for a week or so, although the weather was warm and sunny, there was no sign of him. My mother wondered if he was all right, and eventually she called at the house, taking with her a tin of home made cakes. According to the landlady, there was nothing wrong with the old man, but he refused to budge from his room and wouldn't even dress: just sat in the chair in his dressing-gown for hours on end. My mother went up to the old man's room and tapped on the door. He opened it and looked amazed to see her. She gave him the cakes and asked if he was well. He assured her he was. But he seemed highly embarrassed about something.

'Then why are you staying in your room all the time?' she asked. 'There must be some reason for it, and I'm not leaving here until you tell me what it is.'

He coughed and shuffled, but after some minutes came out with the truth. 'Well, you see, Mrs Dawkin-Jones, it's my trousers.'

'Trousers? What about them?'

'They're worn out.'

'But can't they be mended?'

'I reckon not, mum; they been mended a fair number of times already.'

'May I see?'

Somewhat reluctantly he produced the much patched and darned garments. My mother eyed them expertly. 'Yes, these have certainly had their day. They are your only pair?'

'Yes. And I can't afford a new pair. So I got no choice but to stay in.'

My mother left thoughtfully. She would have liked to give him the money for a new pair, but at that time this was out of the question. And neither my father nor brothers were the same size as the old man, so an old pair of theirs would be useless. Who was there among her relatives about the right size? Ah—Cyril, of course.

My cousin Cyril, son of my mother's sister, Annie, was by then a prosperous Accountant, with a business of his own in Mountstuart Square; and fifteen minutes later my mother was being shown into his office. Her first words surprised him very much: 'Cyril, how many pairs of trousers do you have?'

His reply surprised her equally. As a matter of principle he never kept more than two suits going at one time and the old ones were disposed of immediately he finished with them. 'But I'm fascinated,' he said, 'by this sudden interest of yours in my trousers. Do explain.'

She did so, and he smiled. 'I can't donate any trousers, dear aunt, but I'll gladly buy him a new pair. Will ten shillings be enough?'

Ten shillings was more than enough. Within half an hour a fine new pair of trousers had been purchased and delivered to the old man; and a few minutes later he was sitting outdoors wearing them, as he did for several years. But again, nobody outside our family ever knew where they had come from.

There were literally dozens of such people my mother looked after in various ways. Sunday afternoon was her chief time for visiting. There was old Mrs Hughes, who loved home-made toffee—my mother made a batch for her every Saturday and delivered it on Sunday. There was Mrs Garnett, who was mad about Welsh cakes, and every week a box was taken to her. Old Mrs Desmond liked everything, but especially just being visited, so her parcel was always a surprise.

These Sunday afternoon visits would take about three hours. My mother for years also helped run a girls' sewing class, and once a week they would get together to make things for her famous missionary parcels. This was another work she undertook for several decades. Heaven alone knows how many were sent off over the years, and to how many countries they were sent. Every week a parcel of clothes was made up, and then into the corners my mother would tuck anything that would come in handy, or just be a nice surprise, for a missionary stuck hundreds of miles from civilization—reels of cotton, packets of needles, darning wool, magazines, bottles of sweets, and so on. After packing, if the parcels were going a great distance—China, say, or India—they had to be sewn up in calico, in order to arrive in good condition. Sometimes, the letters of thanks used to be pathetically grateful.

On arriving at Church one Sunday morning, we found, sitting across the aisle from us, a family of missionaries—parents and six children, varying in age from about three to fourteen. For many years they had been working in a remote part of Spain. Now at long last they had come home for a short holiday, and to arrange for the elder children's further education. The most noticeable thing about them was that they wore terribly shabby and old-fashioned clothes.

At lunch my mother was very quiet for a time. Then she burst out with: 'Doesn't it seem awful that after slaving away all those years, the Conways should have to appear in public dressed like that? They look as if they'd floated out of the ark. Someone will have to *do* something.'

Next morning at about nine o'clock she went out armed with a note-book and pencil. Rather cunningly she visited first the office of the most generous businessman known to her at Cardiff docks, and told him she was collecting on behalf of the Conways. He made quite a substantial contribution. She entered it in the book. From there she went the rounds of about a dozen business or professional men, all in Gospel Hall membership. Some had to be leaned on a little, I think, but when they were shown the other entries in the notebook, none had the nerve ultimately to refuse. Eventually, she had enough.

She considered making the Conways a present of the money, but she wanted to be sure it was used to the end for which it had been given, and not for once put by the Conways to the mission work in Spain. Moreover, Mrs Conway, unfortunately but understandably, had little dress sense. So my mother arranged for two respected ladies of the church to take Mrs Conway shopping for herself and the younger children, and for one of the church elders to escort Mr Conway to the best men's outfitters in Cardiff. The two eldest daughters my mother took under her own wing. They were pretty girls with long hair to their waists, one fair, one dark. For one she bought a blue coat, for the other a green. They each had a big, light straw hat, shoes and gloves. However, she could not find dresses for them that quite matched her ideas. No problem—she bought two lengths of material and made the dresses herself. They were in cream vyella, I remember, each with a motif of green or blue to match the coat. On Friday she had to sit up nearly all night in order to finish them by Saturday. But she made it, and on Sunday the transformation in the Conway family had to be seen to be believed.

It was my mother's interest in the welfare of missionaries which led to what was probably her greatest achievement. These missionaries were people who had usually given up everything, including their homes, when they first undertook their vocations, and who relied utterly on contributions from supporters in Britain. There was obviously, therefore, also an obligation to support them when they were at home. To my mother it came to seem more and more unfair that whole families should find themselves constantly in the position of non-paying guests in other people's houses. How nice it would be, she thought, if they could have a place of their own to live, free of charge, for the duration of their stay. Therefore, with the full support of my father, and the assistance of her brother, Rache, she set to work to provide such a home.

First, of course, she obtained the full approval of the Church. Then she again visited the Christian businessmen at the Docks, who were very enthusiastic and generous in their promises. A fund was launched, to which many other people contributed. Eventually enough money was raised and a property—a three-bedroomed terrace house, near a park—was acquired.

Then work started in earnest. Dozens of people volunteered their services—men undertook the repairs and decorations, women made curtains and did other sewing jobs. Even the children helped. Everyone in the Church was asked to give some item, however small, for furnishing and equipping the home. There was not a family that did not contribute. At last everything that could conceivably be needed was obtained. It had been a huge task, and it was quite a day when the house was ready, the larder filled with food, and the first family moved in.

That missionary home is still flourishing today. There are now a number of others, but the one I still tend to think of as 'ours' was the first.

I could not begin to tell of all my mother's activities. Add to everything I have already mentioned the fact that she did all the dressmaking for herself, my three sisters and me; that she played the piano; had a good contralto voice and a great sense of humour—where shall I stop?

Perhaps with the time, many years after my parents had died, when my husband and I drove down to the Docks one summer evening to have a look at the old house. A woman I knew by sight spotted me, smiled, and asked if I remembered her. She'd been brought up in a very poor home and had had a hard life.

'Weren't your parents wonderful people?' she said. 'Do you know what happened once? When I was a little girl, I came here to have a paddle at high tide. I fell down in the water and got soaked from head to foot. I was standing there, crying, when your mother came out and saw me. She said: "You'd better come in and let me dry you off". She took me into your house, gave me a good towelling—and a chocolate —and dressed me in one of your sister's outfits. There was even a petticoat with embroidery round the bottom, threaded with blue ribbon. Then she said: "Now go home and come again tomorrow and I'll have your own clothes all ready for you." I'd never seen such clothes, and my mother had a job that night to get me to undress for bed.'

The lady went on: 'The next day, carrying your sister's clothes done up in a parcel, I went back and your mother had my own clothes washed and ironed and packed ready. I handed her my parcel and she asked: "Did you like those clothes?" Of course, I said yes. "Well," she said, "you'd better keep them." So I went home with two parcels. My mother said later that she'd never seen a child look so happy. I'll never ever forget Mrs Dawkin-Jones for that.'

CHAPTER 7

We hear a lot these days about Victorian hyprocisy, about evil people who presented a facade of religious respectability to cloak their true natures. Numerous novels contain characters of this sort; and usually such characters are depicted as non-conformists.

Well, I saw none of the Victorian era. But I can honestly say that of my elders—my parents, grandparents, aunts, uncles, and their friends among the Brethren—I knew none like this. And they were Victorians to a man and woman. Naturally, they all had their faults. Some of the people one met were pompous or self-important. Some were over-fond of money. Some were probably narrow-minded—though, by the general standards of the day, not so many were even that.

But I am aware of none who were really bad people, clinging to an outward profession of a sham religion. I might, of course, have been deceived by some. But I do not think so. Such people may fool others during their lives, but the truth usually outs after their death. The vast majority of the older people amongst whom I grew up were true believers, who gave unstintingly of their time, and often of their money, in a sincere attempt to spread the Gospel.

No, hypocrites they were not. Harsh, unbending and cruel they were not. And I would not want to have been raised in any other circle.

*   *   *

It was in 1909, according to the records, that my father succeeded my grandfather as Superintendent of the Ebenezer Sunday School. Being a hard worker and good organiser, many other duties connected with the church devolved on him during the years that followed. And naturally, to a large extent, on my mother also.

For isntance, as we had a fairly large house in a pleasant area, it mostly happened that it was we who accommodated visiting speakers. Many of these were missionaries, either retired or home on furlough. Those were the great days of missionary endeavour and there seemed to be a real eagerness among church people to hear stories of mission-aries' work from their own lips. Also, of course, in that pre-television, and almost pre-cinema, era a lantern lecture about China or South America or Central Africa made a good evening's entertainment.

Given this (added to the fact that my father would frequently invite to stay sea captains he had grown friendly with in the course of his work), we virtually never had the house to ourselves and my early memories are of a constant stream of guests. Some we loved having, some we were apathetic about, some, frankly, were pests. But few of them were really dull.

I remember one saintly old evangelist, who rejoiced in the name of Ebsworthy Tapson, and who had been a regular visitor, first to my grandparents, then to us, for years. He, like many others of his kind lived entirely 'by faith'—i.e. taking no stipend or fixed fee, but depending solely on the gifts of the churches he visited. Some evangelists appeared reasonably prosperous, but Mr Tapson was always dreadfully shabbily dressed, in threadbare suit and down-at-heel shoes. It seems that years before, my grandparents had worried a lot about this and eventually they persuaded him to let them buy him a new suit and shoes. Of course, they had to be the best—a bespoke suit and handsewn shoes. Mr Tapson was overjoyed and at the end of his stay left looking very smart. Two or three months later he returned for another visit. To everyone's amazement he was wearing his old suit and shoes again. For the first day or so nobody mentioned this, but at last my grandfather took him aside privately and asked awkwardly: 'Er, by the way, what happened to the suit and shoes? Was anything wrong with them?' Mr Tapson looked embarrassed. 'Peter, you must forgive me. I know it was very wrong of me after your kindness, but I found someone who needed them more than I did, so I gave them to him.' He had given the best away and kept the old. I have met very few people in my life who would do that.

I recall also Mr Haley, an evangelist from Northern Ireland. He'd been born in a poor village near Belfast, in a completely irreligious home, but as a young teenager he had been converted and had immed-iately commenced upon an incredibly rigorous programme of Bible study. He would rise at five every morning for three hours reading before work, in the summer going up into the hills near his home for privacy. By the time he became an itinerant evangelist he knew long passages of the scriptures by heart. He was a wonderful preacher, though tending to be over-emotional at times.

Now, Mr Haley was a big eater, and he became very fat. Eventually, on one of his visits, he explained apologetically that a doctor had put him on a strict diet. He did hope it wouldn't prove too much trouble. He produced a long list of the foods he had to have—many different kinds of fruit, cereals, grated raw vegetables, water biscuits, and so on. My mother said, No, of course, it would be no trouble—and then immediately sent me hurrying off to the shops to stock up. Come tea time that day we all sat down to our usual spread of bread and butter, several kinds of sandwiches, two home-made cakes and a large apple tart. Remembering Mr Haley's appetite, we wondered if he'd be able to stick it out. We were most impressed as he made his way resolutely through his unattractive and spartan fare. When he had finished, which did not take long, he gave a sigh of satisfaction and said: 'Now, might I be having one of those sardine sandwiches, please?' He followed this with several other sandwiches of different varieties, a large helping of apple tart and cream and a slice of fruit cake. So it continued throughout his visit. He honestly believed that as long as he ate the foods laid down in his regimen he could eat what he liked afterwards. The next time Mr Haley came he was as fat as ever and made no mention of his diet. My mother asked him if he wanted special food this time. 'Oh, no,' he said, 'I soon gave up that stupid diet. It was useless—did nothing for me weight at all.'

We were, however, all fond of Mr Haley. My only objection to him was that he was an inveterate tickler. If he had a chance of creeping up behind one unawares he just could not resist. One day I entered the sitting-room to find Mick seated in the corner doing needlework. She looked up.

'Are your hands clean?' she asked.

Thinking she wanted me to hold wool or help her in some other way, I shook my head. 'No, not very.'

'Good. Mine are. So you can made up the fire.'

Outmanouevred, I knelt down on the hearth. Just then, Mr Haley, passing along the hall, spotted me, came in, crept across the room and pounced. Now, if there is one thing I cannot abide it is being tickled.

Within seconds I was almost hysterical and screaming for mercy. But Mr Haley would not stop. However, he had failed to notice Mick. She got up to her feet, approached him from the rear and as he bent over me jabbed her needle home with all her might. It must have gone in an inch. You've never seen an evangelist rise so high in the air. Mick rushed immediately to her room and stayed there until he went out. But Mr Haley did no more tickling.

Perhaps we did not show out venerable guests the respect that was their due. My eldest sister, Lillian, for example, was pestered

The author, centre, with her sisters, Gwen, left, and Lillian.

constantly by one of our visitors—an ex-missionary called Mr Bird. He was a good but rather narrow-minded old Victorian gentleman, who after many years in India, could not at all come to terms with Lillian's modern ways, short skirts and lipstick.

Some idea of his outlook can be gathered from an incident during a visit to my parents of Mr Bird's daughter, when she was a little girl, some years before. One night on a particularly warm evening, my mother went to her room last thing to tuck her in as usual.

'Oh, Auntie,' said Meryl, 'could I have some of these clothes off the bed, please? My feet are as hot as hell.'

'Meryl!' my mother exclaimed, not sure whether to be shocked or to laugh. 'You mustn't say that!'

(In those days 'hell' was a word you did not expect to hear said by anybody in polite society, let alone an eight-year-old missionary's daughter.)

Meryl looked surprised. 'Oh Auntie, don't you know what hell is? It's a terrible place. Daddy's told me all about it. If you're not very good, when you die you go down, down, down into the hands of the Oppressor.'

In the intervening years her father had clearly not mellowed, and from the start of his visit plainly had grave doubts about Lillian's spiritual well-being. Given half an opportunity he would corner her and begin preaching to her earnestly about the sins of the flesh and the snares of the devil. Lillian endured it in silence for a week, then hit back. One day when our parents were out she opened the hall cupboard at a time when she knew Mr Bird would soon be passing through. Then she hid in the recess opposite. When he eventually came unsuspectingly along she suddenly leapt out on him, pushed him as hard as she could, straight into the cupboard and hastily locked the door. Mr Bird began to bang and shout: 'Let me out, you naughty girl, let me out!' 'No,' Lillian called calmly, 'not until you stop buttonholing me and preaching at me. Promise?' And not until the promise was forthcoming was poor Mr Bird released. In fairness to him, he kept his promise. Nor did he tell our parents.

Who else do I recall from those days? Mr Vanson, who was a Lap-lander, an evangelist, and the tallest man I have ever seen. I should think six feet, seven or eight inches would be no exaggeration. He was unique among preachers I have ever heard in that he knelt to pray on the platform. My father was by no means a short man, but Mr Vanson on his knees was nearly as tall as my father standing. The first time Mr Vanson took a bath in our house water cascaded over the edge of the bath and ran down the stairs. He was, though, a charming man, whom we liked very much. He used to talk constantly of his daughter, his 'little Hulda', on whom he doted. She was such a sweet, such a good girl. She had never been out of Lapland, though. He did hope that one day she would be able to come to England. My mother immediately suggested she come to stay with us. Mr Vanson was overjoyed and the arrangements were made. We were all looking forward to seeing this lovely girl. The day arrived—and so did 'little Hulda'.

She turned out to be almost as tall as her father. Moreover, she could speak hardly a word of English—something Mr Vanson had forgotten to mention. My mother had allocated Hulda one of the smaller bedrooms, but the bed in there was clearly not big enough for her.

'She'll never get in it,' my mother said helplessly.

'Never mind the bed,' said Mick, 'she'll never get in the room.'

'It'll be all right,' said Lillian, 'there's a cupboard in the wall opposite the foot of the bed.'

'What's that got to do with it?' my mother asked.

'We'll open the doors and she can rest her feet on the shelves.'

How Hulda was eventually accommodated I don't remember. I think she just slept curled up in a ball. No doubt she was used to this.

Hulda was undoubtedly the most miserable guest we ever had. She did not seem to want to go anywhere or do anything, or even leave the house. For the entire time she was with us she simply sat in the corner of the sitting room, knitting enormous garments. For some inexplicable reason she chose always to sit in a little chair that had at one time usually been mine, but which I'd grown too tall for. When Hulda sat in it her knees reached her chin. She reminded me of the drawings in children's books of pixies sitting on toadstools with their knees jutting up each side of the head. Hulda's knees didn't quite do that, but they were not far short. Perhaps she felt that if she ever fully extended herself she would never succeed in completely compressing herself again and wouldn't be able to get into bed.

We all tried to communicate with Hulda, but it was little use and we breathed a sigh of relief when she departed. For one thing the house seemed much bigger.

I did think that a chronically miserable, never-smiling guest was the worst sort you could have. But no. Someone like Hector, the exact opposite, is even worse. Hector was an irrepressibly cheerful, red-headed Liverpudlian, bearing a striking resemblance to the late Jimmy Hanley. He turned up one night at an evangelistic crusade, of which my father was one of the organisers, and remained in his seat after the rest of the congregation had departed. My father went to speak to him and learned that he had just arrived in Cardiff but had nowhere to stay.

'Oh well, you'd better come home with me, my boy,' said my father, typically.

There followed one of the most miserable periods in our lives. Hector was revoltingly boisterous and happy. If he wasn't singing he was whistling—morning, noon and night. And he was always there. He would be up at night until the last member of the family went to bed—and always the first up in the morning. Mick and I determined that we'd get up before him. Every day we rose a bit earlier—seven, six-thirty, six, five-thirty. But Hector was still down before us, cleaning his shoes—and whistling. 'Hullo, Mick, duck,' he'd shout, giving my sister a slap between the shoulders. 'This is the day that the Lord has made, we will rejoice and be glad in it,' he would bawl.

We didn't, though. Mick and I would wake in the mornings, look at each other, groan and say sadly: 'Hector.'

We never found out anything about Hector's background, why he had come to Cardiff, or what his plans were. He didn't appear to be looking for a job. After a month or so, when it really seemed he was intending to stay for ever, he just disappeared, never, thankfully, to return.

The only genuine, if minor, celebrity, whom we ever entertained was Dr Scofield, the editor of the famous Reference Bible, who came to preach at Ebenezer one weekend. I wish I could say I have vivid recollections of his wisdom and learning. Alas, only one memory remains. For tea on the Sunday my mother supplied her usual spread. Dr Scofield, being, for a Biblical scholar, seemingly strangely ignorant of Luke 10. 8, suddenly asked if he might have a boiled egg. Now, he was accompanied on his visit by a lady secretary, who then also asked politely if she might have a boiled egg too. He turned to her irritably. 'Certainly not,' he said. 'Why have you got to ask for a boiled egg, just because I did? What's the matter with you?'

CHAPTER 8

One of our church's unforgettable characters I shall call simply Alf. An electrician by trade, Alf was one of this world's true originals. His uniqueness, I think, lay in the fact that he was a man who would always come out with exactly what was on his mind. In many people this trait would cause offence, but Alf was such a genial character, so free of malice, so full of good will to all the world, and so utterly sincere that he got away with it. Even in his prayers.

When praying in public he would completely forget that anyone else was present. It was just himself and God. I wish I could remember all his sayings, but a few have always stuck in my mind.

For instance, once during a long, hot summer, he prayed for rain, adding, as an afterthought: 'Not, as it were, cats and dogs, Lord, but just enough to lay the dust.'

Again, one Christmas time he was giving thanks for the Nativity and acknowledging how cold and dark and uncomfortable the stable at Bethlehem must have been. A pause, then: 'And, oh Lord, the smell!' This became a sort of catchphrase in our house for years afterwards and I still say it if confronted with an unpleasant aroma from any source.

It often fell to Alf to read the notices or announcements at the evening services. He was unique in that he did not go onto the platform to do this, nor just stand on the floor in front of it. He would scramble up onto the front pew. Then he'd beam around and begin. He could never resist adding comments of his own. Once he had been asked to draw attention to the poor attendance at the weekly young men's meeting. Having dutifully done so, 'Perhaps they ought to get some young women there,' he added, 'that ought to do the trick.'

On another occasion, having to read out details of a series of services to be held at a local, rather sleepy Methodist church, called the Forward Movement Hall, he added, *sotto voce*, but loud enough for everyone to hear: 'Forward Movement? Backward push, I call it.'

Yet, as I say, he never gave offence. Who else but Alf could have got away with saying jovially to an elderly, grim-faced lady in the porch one night, when the rain was teeming down: "Evening, Mrs Fish. Just the weather for you, isn't it?'

But it was in speaking to children that Alf really came into his own. The Sunday School teachers used to take it in turns to address the whole school for about ten minutes at the end of the afternoon. And Alf's turns ('turn' not being an inappropriate word) were on their own.

I remember his object lessons to this day. One time he asked for a volunteer to come on to the platform. When a small boy did so, Alf produced a reel of cotton, tied his arms to his side with a single loop of it, then told him to try and break it—which, of course, the boy did without trouble. Then he was tied with two loops, with the same result. When tied with five he had a little difficulty, but eventually broke free. Finally, Alf encircled him about fifteen times. The boy, naturally, was quite unable to break away. As an illustration of how minor faults and bad habits can grow insidiously until they take control of a person it was more effective than any number of stories or homilies.

Again, I recall a time when throughout his talk he had resting on the rail by him the reddest, juciest-looking apple I had ever seen. I think the mouth of every child in the place was watering as they gazed at it. Then at the end Alf took out a knife and carefully cut the apple in half, to reveal that it was bad to the core. Beautiful on the outside, rotten within. The lesson drawn from this does not need pointing by me. I still do not know how he knew that apple was bad. He was quite capable of cutting a dozen in half until he found a bad one, then sticking it together again with glue.

I think, however, that his most memorable performance was an illustration of the story of the feeding of the multitude with five loaves and two fishes. Alf told the story from the point of view of the lad who supplied the fishes. First he had to catch them. The platform became the bank of a river, as he first sat with his feet dangling over the side, and then lay flat on his stomach, trying to scoop up imaginary fishes with a net. He'd 'catch' one, lift it from the net, try to hold it, wriggling and slippery, and 'accidentally' drop it back in. I can almost see those non-existent fishes today. (Incidentally, it wasn't only on children that he used object lessons. He was once seen, prior to addressing a women's meeting, carrying literally scores of vases, jars and urns from his car into the church. They were to illustrate all the various Bible stories in which such objects featured—and there are a surprising lot of them. Alf had borrowed them from all his friends and neighbours and the main problem lay, I believe, in getting them all back to their rightful owners afterwards.)

Alf was about the only Sunday School worker I've ever known who used positively to encourage the children to make a noise. As Superintendent in later life (he succeeded my father), he used to divide the school into teams—boys versus girls, or left versus right—and get them to vie with each other to see who could sing the hymns or choruses the loudest. Once, when somebody mildly remonstrated with him about the appalling cacophony that used to issue forth from the church, he beamed. 'As singing it may not be up to much, but they're making a joyful noise unto the Lord, just like the Bible tells them to.'

★   ★   ★

The great day of the Sunday School year was the Whitsun Treat, and I think Alf enjoyed it more than any of the children. While they were lining up outside to march to the station he would be there, wearing a funny hat, carrying a huge, multi-coloured beach umbrella, running up and down, waving to the neighbours watching from their houses, acting the clown and keeping the kids amused—and together.

At the Whitsun Treat.

82

For others, including my father, the Treat was a more anxious time. Days beforehand he would start worrying about the weather. On the morning of Whit Monday he'd be up at about six o'clock constantly going outside, staring at the sky. He was a wonderful forecaster and often when the sun was shining out of an expanse of cloudless blue and everyone else was sure it was set fair, he would slowly shake his head and pronounce it 'foxy'. Sure enough, within an hour or two it would be raining.

Fortunately, for the Whitsun Treat it mostly seemed to be fine and, in my recollection, very hot. I remember only a couple of wet days— and they were very wet ones.

The children had to be at the church by eight a.m. They would nearly all turn up in sparkling new (or their newest) clothes, the girls in floral dresses, the boys in grey shorts, held up by belts with snake buckles. Both sexes invariably wore white plimsolls, known locally as 'daps'. There would be a tremendous air of excitement. The children had been looking forward to it for months. For many of the poorer ones it was their only outing of the year, and certainly their only train ride. They would have to line up in the aisles, go into the vestry and have the backs of their hands rubber-stamped with the words 'Eben-ezer Hall Sunday School'. This was their pass onto the train. While they were waiting somebody—usually Alf—would be leading them in singing. The noise would be quite terrible. Then would come the assembly in the street and the ten minute march to the station, behind a big banner. The special train would be waiting and the children would pile in.

When I was little the train journey was for me a very worrying one. My father would be the last to get on, standing on the platform until every child was aboard and then swinging himself on, guard-like, after the train was moving. But I could hardly ever get close enough to the windows, jammed with shouting children, actually to see him do this. And every year I worried the whole way in case he'd been left behind. It was only a ten mile journey and there were plenty of other trains, so it would hardly have been a major disaster if he had been. Nevertheless, it was always a tremendous relief to me when we reached our destination and I saw him safely arrived.

After we had detrained there would be another ten minute's march to the field. The young male teachers would have been camping there for a couple of days, and the large marquee would already have been erected, together with the tea, sweet and ice cream stalls, the tracks laid out ready for the races, the swings and slides put up and all the other hundred and one necessary preparations made.

On arrival the children would all sit down on the grass (if there had been any rain a big tarpaulin would have been laid and if it was actually raining they would be herded into the marquee) and served milk and buns. After this they would usually stampede to the stalls and spend their pennies and tuppences. When later on I became a teacher myself with a class of girls, they would all wish to buy me something, and they invariably seemed to choose the same thing—a kind of concoction of Turkish delight and nuts, a bar of which I think cost a halfpenny. Within ten minutes half a dozen of these bars would have been thrust into my hands. 'I bought this for you, miss'. I had to spend much time during the day surreptitiously disposing of them to other children.

After this the games and the races would start—all the usual things; three-legged, egg and spoon, obstacle races; cricket, rounders and so on. For those who preferred it there were the swings and slides.

During this time the older people used to sit round the big marquee in deck chairs, watching and gossiping. I remember being at some time in the day expected to go along the line, paying my respects and being kissed by most of the ladies, which I intensely disliked.

If the worst happened and it did rain all the activities would be held in the marquee—party games, quizzes, spelling bees, and so on.

Fairly early in the afternoon tea would be served. There would be two or three great urns, bread and butter, and several kinds of slab cake—rich fruit, cherry or Madeira. The children would get through enormous quantities. At about five a short service would be held and at five-thirty it would be back to the station—a more subdued, far less spick and span bunch of children than the ones who had marched in the other direction eight hours before . . .

The highlight of the summer for my family, though, was not the Whitsun Treat but our annual holiday in Porthcawl. Aunt Bess (the headmistress) owned a lovely big house there and every year she

84

The Sunday School teachers. Lewis Dawkin-Jones, Superintendent, sitting, fourth from left. The author second row from back, seventh from left. 'Alf' in policeman's helmet.

would let her three sisters have it for a month each. My mother would take Len, Mick and me (the older members of the family had by then graduated to holdays with friends). My father could only manage a couple of weekends and possibly, if he was lucky, one full week.

We would set off on the train, in the highest spirits. The oddest thing about the journey now seems the fact that from about the half way mark we children would be hanging out of the carriage windows, craning our necks for our first excited glimpse of the sea. Yet we lived by the sea and saw it every day! Somehow, though, this sea—albeit still the Bristol Channel—was different: a holiday sea.

There are some fine beaches in Wales, the grandest probably in the north and west—Llandudno, Rhossili, Tenby, etc. For me, the best in the south are at Porthcawl. There are two: Coney Beach and Rest Bay. Aunt Bess's house—set well back from the road, with large gardens front and rear—was opposite Coney Beach. That end of Porthcawl has now been spoilt by the funfairs and general air of candyflossishness. But in those days the only holidaymakers' facility was the row of bathing boxes. We could leave our front door, cross the road, run over the stretch of lovely white sandhills, dotted with loganberry bushes, and where it was possible to lose yourself for hours—and there was the glorious beach.

That month seemed endless and the weather always fine. I suppose it must have rained sometimes, but I don't remember it. We spent hours in the water, Len and Mick swimming and me trying to. For this was something that although a dozen people tried to teach me, I never mastered. Except, that is, on one occasion. I used to manage quite well with water wings and one day was splashing along quite happily when I suddenly discovered the wings were no longer with me. They had come off! I was swimming! There was a moment's exhilaration—then fear.

At that point my new-found skill deserted me. Like the Apostle Peter, walking on the water, as soon as I lost faith, I started to sink. Like Peter, too, I cried out and somebody rescued me. After that, it was back to the water wings. Though these themselves nearly brought about my premature death once, when they slipped down to my knees, causing me to nose dive. My head was suddenly under the water, with apparently no way of getting back. I would certainly have drowned if, again, someone had not been on hand to save me.

My mother could not swim either—or only very little. But she managed without water wings. She had learned simply to float—wading out until the water was nearly up to her chin, then just relaxing and letting herself fall backwards. She would then bob around in the water for ages, quite happily. It was perfectly satisfactory so long as there were no strong currents, for of course, she had no control over her movements. Once I remember she embarrassed herself very much —but amused him no end—by floating backwards into the stomach of a very large, fat man.

We made our own amusements during those long, hot summers. There were no pierrots or dodgems or penny arcades, no cinemas or even restaurants. But nobody, I am sure ever enjoyed holidays more.

Sunday, the so-called 'day of rest', I look back on now as probably the most exhausting day of the week. We always had to be up early to prepare the vegetables for dinner and put the roast in the oven. Then we'd each get our own breakfast—not cooked, but everybody helping themselves to whatever cold food they fancied. (I always liked a banana and bread and butter.) After this we would change into our

Sunday best for morning service. It was about twenty minutes' walk to Ebenezer—or for me, a ten minute run. This because I was nearly always late and the others left before me. Very occasionally, if one was in luck, one could catch a tram part of the way, but they were few and far between on Sundays. So I would usually arrive hot and panting at the church and spend the first quarter of an hour of the service getting my breath back.

Ebenezer Gospel Hall.

At the close, it would be a fast walk home to change into old clothes and prepare, serve and eat dinner—rarely for less than ten. Immediately lunch was over we would have to change back into our best clothes for Sunday School at 2.30.

Then it was a repeat performance: hurry home, change again and help serve a large, laid tea, of the sort I have described earlier—again for perhaps ten or a dozen people. It occurs to me now that, after a heavy lunch a few hours before, nobody really wanted this; a cup of tea and biscuit or piece of cake would have been quite adequate. However, we were only doing the conventional thing.

After tea had been cleared away we would change once more for the evening service at six-thirty. Then it would be home for the last time —having spent two hours of the day walking to and from church—for a final change of clothes before preparing a light supper—perhaps cold meat, pickles and bread and butter.

The rest of the day was our own, and if I was lucky I might be able to put my feet up with a book for an hour or so before bed. By that time I really felt I needed it.

There were some extremely 'tough eggs'—of both sexes—among the Sunday School pupils. I remember a boy—the one who had been tied up by Alf—who made life such a misery for his teacher (even putting a drawing pin on his seat when he stood up for a hymn, and on which he scored a direct hit when sitting down) that the poor man threatened to resign if the boy was not expelled. But my father was adamant.

'I'm sorry, Bob,' he said, 'I don't want to lose you, but no child will ever be turned away or turned out while I'm Superintendent of this Sunday School.' That was the end of the matter.

I became a teacher very reluctantly. I was one of the newest members of the girls' senior Bible class, which was held in a separate room at the same time as the Sunday School. One afternoon my father came in, whispered to the leader for a moment, then addressed the class:

'Girls, one of the teachers hasn't turned up today. I need a volunteer to take her class—nine-year-old girls.'

I glanced interestedly round the twenty or so young women present, wondering which of them would be the first to volunteer.

They all suddenly became very busy: rummaging in their bags, wiping their noses, or devoutly reading their Bibles or hymn books—anything to avoid catching his eye.

'Come along, girls. Surely one of you will help out?'

There was still no response. My father sighed, located me and beckoned with one finger. 'Winn.'

I gave a gasp. 'Me?'

'Yes, and hurry up, my dear. They're waiting.'

There was no escape. My heart in my mouth I followed him out to the main school. When I saw the class I was to take my spirits sank even lower. They were notorious, regularly sending their middle-aged teacher into semi-hysterics, so that she had to be taken out by someone and given drinks of water. I wasn't really surprised she had thrown in the towel. One girl in particular, by the name of Nellie, was the ringleader.

Nervously I sat down, and hastily racking my brains, launched into the story of Esther. I tried to make it as interesting as I could, describing the riches of the king's court, the jewellery, the gold dishes, the gorgeous gowns of the queen.

For a few minutes the girls were silent, captured mainly I think by the novelty of a new teacher, but then gradually the whispering, giggling, face-pulling and jostling broke out again. I soon realized that nobody was taking the slightest notice of me. I didn't really know what to do. A Sunday School teacher is not in the same position as an ordinary school teacher: he or she cannot keep the children in after school or give them lines—let along hit them! And as I have said, explusion was absolutely vetoed. The only sanction was to warn them they would not be allowed to come to the Whitsun Treat. But this threat had been made hundreds of times—since I was in the infants' class at least, and probably much longer—without once being enforced. It had thus rather lost its terror. So how did one keep order?

I just ploughed on with Esther and Vashti and Haman and Mordecai, until Nellie, who in spite of my constant commands of 'Be quiet, Nellie,' had been chattering continually to her next door neighbour, calmly reached up and removed the hat from the head of the girl on her other side—a well-behaved and rather timid child. The hat was obviously new, much prized and covered with artificial flowers of every kind. Nellie now proceeded to try to 'pick' these. The owner, too frightened to complain, stared on in horror.

I quickly removed the hat from Nellie's grasp, returned it, little harmed, to its owner, and leaned back.

'Well, Nellie, as you know this story so well. I think you'd better finish it for us.'

Nellie stared at me insolently. 'What d'you mean, miss?'

'You finish the story.'

'I don't know it.'

'Oh, I'm sorry. I thought, as you weren't bothering to listen, you must have heard it before.'

There was a little titter from the rest of the class and I was emboldened. 'Well, it doesn't matter. Tell us another, instead.'

'Dunno any.'

'Oh, surely you do. You've been coming to Sunday School for years now. You must have heard hundreds. Any one.'

Nellie glowered at me silently. I pushed home my advantage. 'Now, Nellie, you're just being modest. We all know you're such a good talker. So carry on.'

Ebenezer Infants Class, 1950.

90

And I folded my arms. There was silence. All the girls were now staring at Nellie, who slowly went red. I let half a minute pass before relenting.

'Well, perhaps Nellie wasn't ready. We'll give her a week to prepare a story. She can tell it next Sunday. Unless, of course, she really shows she would rather listen to mine.'

For the rest of that afternoon I had no further trouble and at the end really felt quite pleased with myself. My father was impressed too.

'In fact,' he said, 'I think it would be a good idea if I switched Mrs Price to one of the more senior classes—there are several of the older ladies who will be glad of a rest—and let you take the class permanently.'

That was how I became a Sunday School teacher—wishing earnestly that I had let Nellie and Co. run riot the entire afternoon, thus proving myself utterly unsuitable for the work. However, I was stuck with them. I won't say I had no further trouble with them, but I gradually won them over.

And it never occurred to me to try the tactics of Jean, a friend of ours, who found herself in the same position—having to take over an unruly class, in her case of boys. The first week she seemed able to do nothing with them at all. But the second week they were as good as gold—listening in perfect silence.

'How on earth did you manage it?' I asked her later.

She looked round cautiously, then whispered in my ear: 'I told them that if they promised to be good I'd read them a "Just William" story today.'

CHAPTER 9

It is a fact that people and things one accepts at face value as a child take on a different appearance when one looks back on them in later years.

Consider my mother's brother, our Uncle Henry. He seemed a most generous man, who was always bringing us food. Often it was of the luxurious kind—chicken (not so plentiful and cheap then as it is now) or whole salmon. But in retrospect I realize that he was always there to help eat it—and usually accompanied by some business acquaintance. The fact is that his offices were only about a mile away from us, whereas he lived in Whitchurch, to the north of Cardiff. So if he wanted to give a customer lunch (and be sure it was a good one) at a fraction of the price he would pay in a high class restaurant, it was by far the best plan to take him to his sister's house. All he had to do was drop off something for the main course the previous day and rely on 'old Lyd' to do the rest. If it wasn't lunch he would frequently 'drop in' mid-morning, often with a customer in tow, and expect to be given coffee.

Again, Uncle Henry had a passion for larva bread—the Welsh 'delicacy' made from seaweed, which in its uncooked state looks like opaque, black jelly. I find the taste of it quite repulsive. It has to be fried and the smell of it cooking is something I would prefer not to try and describe. Regularly Uncle Henry would turn up with a parcel of the stuff—and my mother would be expected to cook it for him. It was usually the signal for a general exodus by the family. And the reason he brought it to our house was that his wife, Emily, wouldn't have the stuff in hers.

'Aunt Em' was the most houseproud woman I have ever met. Everything in her home gleamed. Her poor maid had to do things over and over again. 'Mary, did you polish that this morning?' Aunt Em would ask, pointing to some spotless, shining ornament or piece of furniture.

'I don't remember, mum,' the silly girl would say.

'Better do it again, to make sure.'

Aunt Em took up all the staircarpets in her house because they were getting dirty and replaced them with newspapers; and Uncle Henry had to put on carpet slippers inside the front door—and even then sit with his feet on a newspaper.

This trait, however, applied only to her own house. On the occasions when they came to stay with us for a day or two (whenever Uncle Henry felt like waking up to a sea view), Aunt Em would stay in bed half the morning, eating toffees and throwing the papers on the floor, where she would leave them for somebody else to pick up.

She owned a black pomeranian dog, a nasty, pampered, snapping creature, which she used to feed on fresh chicken and strawberries and cream. The only time I ever saw her moved was when the animal died. 'Poor little Blacky's passed away,' she sobbed to my mother. All in all, it was perhaps not surprising that Uncle Henry preferred to eat many of his meals at our house.

Another example of his particular kind of generosity was that on several occasions he took Len, Mick and me on quite expensive seaside holidays. But we soon found that every moment of our time was mapped out for us. We had hardly any opportunities just to do what we wanted to.

The author, right, with 'Mick' and Len.

He could also be incredibly touchy. For example, Aunt Em hailed from Bridgewater in Somerset, and one year when I was in my teens I went with a party of young people to Bridgewater on 5th November. Bridgewater in those days was famous—or notorious—for its Guy Fawkes celebrations. I discovered too late that everyone in the town seemed to go mad. I found myself in a seething mass of people, singing and shouting; fireworks were being thrown from all directions, bangers and crackerjacks going off under your feet and almost in your face. I had really never been so frightened in my life and was frankly very relieved eventually to get away from the place.

Next time Uncle Henry called, he asked how I'd enjoyed my trip to Bridgewater.

'Oh,' I began, 'what a ghastly place . . .'

Uncle Henry leapt to his feet. His face was red. 'How dare you!' he shouted.

I stared at him in amazement. 'What do you mean?'

'I take that as a calculated insult to my wife!' he yelled. 'You *know* Em was born in Bridgewater. And you call it a ghastly place Impudence!'

'I only meant ghastly on Guy Fawkes night . . .' I started, but he wouldn't let me finish.

'I shall not stay here a moment longer!' And he stormed out of the room and out of the house.

I looked helplessly at my mother. 'What did I say wrong?'

'Nothing,' she told me. 'He's an idiot.'

'Should I chase after him and apologise?'

'Certainly not. Just ignore him. He'll get over it eventually.'

As it happened it was some time before I saw Uncle Henry again, and on that occasion my technique was to pretend the incident had never occurred. Actually, he did seem a little abashed at first, which was the nearest thing one would ever geto to an apology from him.

Uncle Henry would often go overboard for some passing craze or fad—would hear a lecture or read an article about a new idea, and be quite carried away by it. One time when, for some reason without Aunt Em, he was staying with us, he had to be up early the next morning to start on a long business trip. My mother casually mentioned that there was an alarm clock in his room.

He shook his head. 'Shan't need it—shan't even set it,' he said firmly.

'Oh, why not?'

'I shall wake by faith.'

'What do you mean?'

'I shall simply repeatedly tell myself before I go to sleep that I shall wake at six-thirty. I shall then wake at six-thirty on the dot. Anybody can learn to do it. It's all a question of belief.'

'All the same,' said my mother, 'I think I'd better look in and make sure you're awake.'

'No, Lyd, there's absolutely no need. I shall be awake.'

'Well, if you're certain . . .'

'Quite certain.'

'Very well.'

At seven a.m. the next day my father said uneasily: 'Look, do you think we ought to call Henry?'

'No,' replied my mother. 'He said quite definitely we weren't to. For once I'm going to take him at his word.'

When Uncle Henry eventually stumbled downstairs at eight-thirty he was furious. 'It was a most important business meeting! How am I going to explain? Why didn't you call me?'

He did not like being reminded of waking by faith.

Yes, Uncle Henry liked his sleep. And whenever possible he had to go to sleep immediately he felt tired. What is more, he could sleep virtually anywhere. (In a strange town, if the urge to go to sleep came over him, he would often pop into the first cinema he came to and settle down for a hour or two.) This trait and his liking of organizing people are both demonstrated in the incident of the northern conference.

Uncle Henry drove thousands of miles a year on business. He had a big old Ford, that would probably hold six in comfort. One year, during the winter months some big convention or conference was arranged in the north of England, which Uncle Henry decided to attend. So did quite a number of his friends and relations. This presented a fine opportunity for Uncle Henry to display his fabled largesse. For the next couple of weeks, whenever he met anyone who planned to go to the conference but had not yet made travelling arrangements, he insisted they come with him.

When the day arrived no fewer than eight men turned up at the house, all expecting a comfortable ride to the north. Uncle Henry was not a big embarrassed. 'Pile in,' he insisted. 'Plenty of room.'

For him, as driver, of course, there was plenty of room. But for the others . . . However, by now it was too late to make alternative arrangements. So pile in they did. For the first couple of hours things, though bad enough, were bearable. Then, however, it grew dark and the driver started to get sleepy. He immediately pulled into a lay-by.

'I'm going to have a nap,' he said. He leant back in his seat and went fast asleep, leaving his eight passengers, far too uncomfortable to sleep themselves, just to sit, without heating, in the dark, until he decided to drive on. He slept for two solid hours.

One of the passengers on that trip was a future brother-in-law of mine. He told me that in those pre-motorway, pre-service area and pre-car heater days, it was the worst trip he ever had. And he'd been through the first world war.

Just as Uncle Henry liked to be able to sleep whenever he felt like it, so he liked to be able to eat the moment he felt hungry. When driving alone he would always have something edible on the passenger seat and help himself from it at frequent intervals. (In the summer it would usually be a couple of punnets of strawberries and an open bag of castor sugar for dipping them.) Or somewhere in one of his pockets there was nearly always some kind of food.

On one occasion he was driving my sister Gwenneth somewhere when, to his intense annoyance, his car broke down and they had to take a bus. It was very crowded, with just a couple of aisle seats on top, one at the front, one at the back. Uncle Henry ensconsed Gwen in the rear seat and made his way to the front. He sat down, gazed around—and soon began to get bored. He was not used to riding on buses and he didn't like not being in control. Just for something to do he started to search through his pockets—and to his delight found a veal and ham pie. From another pocket he took a clasp knife and proceeded to cut himself a large chunk.

In the rear seat Gwen watched horrified. She was a very sensitive person, kindly, and by far the most genuinely generous I have ever

Gwen, left, and Lillian.

known. But she was also a stickler for the most punctiliously correct behaviour on every occasion. And one did not eat in public—especially on buses. It seemed that everyone on the top of this bus could see what Uncle Henry was doing. She hoped devoutly that they thought she and this awful man had just happened to get on at the same stop.

But at that moment Uncle Henry suddenly remembered his niece. She might be hungry. He turned, held the pie in the air and called loudly:

'Gwen—want a piece of pie?'

Gwen went bright red and ignored him. And Uncle Henry realized her embarrassment. He got to his feet and walked a few steps down the aisle, still holding out the pie. 'Come on, love, 'ave a bit of 'Arris's veal 'n' 'am pie.'

At this Gwen rushed for the stairs. She took the next bus on her own.

'He did it deliberately, just to humiliate me,' she said furiously later. 'And he purposely dropped his aitches. I hate him. I'll never speak to him again.'

And she didn't, for all of two weeks.

I do not want to give a completely bad impression of Uncle Henry. He was capable of genuine kindness and would go to endless trouble to help anyone who really needed it.

One day he arrived at his office in the morning to find four children sitting tearfully on the step. They were the family of his brother George—the one who had been killed a couple of years before by being struck with an anchor. Their mother, Annette, always a somewhat flighty creature, had, it seemed, suddenly got sick of caring for them and had departed for London, stopping just to drop them off at her brother-in-law's office first. (She never returned.)

Uncle Henry was quite undaunted. He took the one girl to her grandmother's house, one of the boys to his sister Miriam's, and another to us. There was no question of any of us being asked 'Could you take this child?' We were just told we had to. The third boy, be it admitted, Uncle Henry took into his own house. It was, of course, cruel to separate the children, who had already lost both their father and mother. But there was nothing my parents could do about it;

obviously it would have been impossible for them to take in all four children.

However, the arrangement was to last only a month or so. Uncle Henry arrived to announce that he had found places for the girl and two of the boys at a private orphanage for the children of Royal and Merchant Navy Officers near Reading.

'*Two* of the boys?' my mother said.

'Em and I have decided to keep Ronnie,' Uncle Henry announced proudly. 'We're going to adopt him.'

He and Em had had no children, and it was suspected Em had never wanted them—that they would make the house much too untidy. My mother wondered if she was as pleased with the plan as Uncle Henry obviously was.

It seemed hard for the other children to be sent to an orphanage while their brother was adopted; but on the other hand, it was probably better for the three of them to be together.

For Ronnie, however, the transformation in his life after his mother's departure must have been shattering. This was at the height of Uncle Henry's prosperity—and nothing was too good for his new son. He had his own room, a wardrobe of top quality clothes and the best food. He was showered with presents—and, in fact, thoroughly spoilt.

But—only by Uncle Henry. For Aunt Em, from what we heard, was indeed not so enthusiastic. Whatever the reason, she did not get on very well with children, and was, shall we say, rather 'cool' towards Ronnie. The poor boy must have been completely confused and no doubt often thought that his brothers and sister were the lucky ones, after all.

Then, after a year or two, we heard out of the blue that Ronnie was to join them at the orphanage. We never learnt the reason: whether it was Aunt Em's decision; whether Uncle Henry had just tired of the novelty of having a son; whether Ronnie had blotted his copybook in some way—and if so whether he might have done it deliberately. (He was a wily child and might well have decided that *he* had had enough of Henry and Em.)

However, off he went and the chapter was closed. The only thing to add is that it must have been a fine orphanage. All four children emerged from it years later well-educated, beautifully spoken and impeccably mannered; and all did very well for themselves. Which is a sort of happy ending to the episode.

I have mentioned Uncle Henry's sudden enthusiasms for passing crazes. He was also something of a health crank, always discovering miracle cures or wonderful new quack healers.

One day he turned up at our house, full of praise for a marvellous bone-setter or manipulator he had found.

'Just a working man—boilermaker—but a natural gift. Done wonders for my arthritic knee. I know, Lewis.' He turned to my father: 'I'll bring him along to have a look at your toe.'

For years my father had had a permanently stiff big toe joint. It could be painful, but he had learned to live with it. 'Oh no, Henry, I don't think I'll bother,' he said.

But it was useless trying to argue with Uncle Henry in that mood, and it was arranged for the wonder man to call. He came a few days later, an unprepossessing, taciturn individual, who did not inspire confidence. For about half an hour he massaged and manupulated my father's toe, and at the end of the session it was certainly more painful than it had been for years. However, the man insisted it would take time to effect a complete cure, and he departed, leaving behind a bottle of his own patent liniment—the main ingredient of which was amonia—giving strict instructions that my father massage some of it into his toe first thing every morning. My father put the bottle on his bedside table so that he would not forget.

Now, my mother used to make her own cough mixture. Unlike most medicines it tasted very nice and had a most warming and soothing effect. To my great regret I never learned the recipe, but I know that it contained ipecacuanha, licorice and a tiny amount of laudanum. She used to make several pints at a time and then put it up into medicine bottles. It was my father's habit to keep a bottle by the side of his bed during the winter months, for, if he'd been out all day during a force nine gale and lashing rain he tended to cough a little at night. It was his habit, whenever he had to take any kind of medicine, just to down a big swig whenever he felt like it—no 'two teaspoons three times a day' for him. And he was convinced that if he forgot it during the day, it was perfectly all right to make up for it by swallowing half a tumblerful at night. Though, with his own personal bottle of cough mixture, he didn't bother with a tumbler. If he woke up coughing in the night he would reach out in the dark, uncork the bottle, and half empty it straight down his throat.

The first Mick and I knew of something wrong was when we were woken suddenly by the sound of hideous groans coming from our parents' bedroom. We scrambled out of bed and in a panic rushed in. My father was lying on the floor, gasping and choking, his hands clasped to his throat. My mother, bending over him, white-faced, looked up as we burst in. She wasted not a second.

'He's swallowed the liniment. Get some warm water—quickly— and lots of it.'

We charged out, running into Len, and explaining to him in a few gasping words what had happened. We dashed to the kitchen, turned on all four jets of the cooker and put on the kettle and three saucepans. In a couple of minutes Len was running upstairs with the first lot. Seconds later he was back.

'More!' he shouted.

So, for the next quarter of an hour Mick and I heated pan after pan of water, while Len ran to and from my parents' room with jugs. Meanwhile, a friend who had been staying with us had got his car out and gone for the doctor.

In the bedroom my mother was pouring glass after glass of tepid water into my father's mouth. The trouble was that the liniment must have contained, as well as the ammonia, some strong sedative. For my father, not after the first ten minutes apparently in much pain, wanted only to sleep. Lying back, his eyes half closed, he kept murmuring: 'Leave me alone—must sleep—leave me alone,' and trying to push the glass away.

My mother, however, knew that sleep could be fatal. She continued virtually to force the water between his lips. At last the emetic had its effect, and a few minutes later the doctor arrived.

When the doctor emerged from my father's room later he was shaking his head crossly. 'I don't know,' he said, 'why this lady'—he indicated my mother—'keeps wasting my time by sending for me.'

We gasped. Then he smiled. 'She doesn't need me. Whenever anybody's ill or had an accident she's always done absolutely the right thing before I ever get here.'

He was serious. 'She's saved your father's life, there's no doubt about it. He'll be all right now. Of course the lining of his stomach has been badly burned.'

'What do we do about that?' my mother asked wearily.

'White of egg. He must take nothing else for at least two weeks.'

As we at last clambered back into bed at about five a.m., Mick said suddenly: 'Gosh, we're going to have to buy an awful lot of eggs.'

But we did not have to buy a single extra egg. For in no time news of my father's accident and of the prescribed treatment got out. And immediately the eggs started to arrive. Three or four times a day. In dozens, half dozens; in threes and fours and pairs they were delivered to the door. In bowls and boxes and bags, clasped in children's hands. The gatekeeper at the entrance to the Roath Dock, who kept three or four hens in his back yard, brought one egg every day without fail.

I don't think I had ever realized until that time in how high esteem my father was held.

Meanwhile, the rest of us practically drowned under a sea of egg yolk. We had them scrambled—in omelettes—in custard tarts—in puddings of every kind. We tried to give them away; but it is not as easy to give away egg yolks as it is whole eggs: they have to be carried through the streets in bowls or jars; and besides it would have seemed ungrateful to appear too anxious to get rid of them. But by the time my father had recovered none of us wanted to see another egg for months.

Yes, recover he did—slowly. One of the most alarming symptoms had been a swelling of his head to about half as big again as its usual size. But this too, as well as his mouth and stomach, gradually returned to normal.

He had had some minor heart trouble a year or so previously, and one day when he was on the mend I said to him: 'Well, they say ammonia's a heart stimulant, so perhaps it will do you good.'

'A most drastic treatment, my dear,' he said dryly. 'But do you know what really annoys me?'

'No,' I said. 'What?'

'My blessed toe is as bad as ever.'

CHAPTER 10

When I was young we always had marvellous Christmases. The house was invariably packed, as even after my elder sisters married and moved away they would not miss coming home for the holiday, together with their husbands and later their children. Extra beds were put in every room and the house was constantly seething with activity: presents being wrapped, decorations, holly and mistletoe being put up, the tree being dressed—and always something special being cooked. There were parties somewhere nearly every day.

My mother's Christmas started in early September. She had many friends and relations, all of whom had to be remembered, but with money never plentiful, she could not just go and buy dozens of presents. So she made them.

She made lavender bags in pretty pastel shades of organdie, tied with ribbons to match. She made fancy coat-hangers, buying plain wooden ones, binding them with cotton wool and then covering them in good quality material, such as figured velvet, remnants of which could be bought inexpensively; with a little gathering along the tops, and the hooks bound by ribbon, they made most popular presents and I know of people who are using theirs to this day.

Again, my mother would make beautiful dressing-table pin cushions. It was possible then to buy little china figures of ladies—or at least of their top halves. Mother would make a container of ticking, stuff it with bran and join it to the holes provided in the base of the figure. Then she would make a frilly skirt and fit it over the bran bag, so that the lady looked as though she were wearing a bustle. When completed, they were really very attractive.

In addition, mother embroidered tray cloths, crocheted doilies and knitted or sewed all sort of other little items. All these presents would be wrapped in tissue paper and put away in drawers—and it was then time to start tackling everything on the home front. And everything was a lot.

The first big job was the Christmas puddings. These would be made in October and every year mother cooked at least a dozen. We all had to help in the preparation—stoning raisins, blanching almonds, cutting up candied peel, etc. The ingredients were mixed in a huge enamel bowl, which was never used for anything else. Everybody had to have a stir, 'for luck', and then the mixture was put into basins; greaseproof paper was stretched across the top; and finally the whole basin was wrapped in calico, bound tightly with twine (my father's contribution, this) and the surplus material brought to the top and fastened loosely with a safety pin, to make a sort of handle. The puddings were then simmered for twenty-four hours in the kitchen boiler. When they were ready, one was immediatgely put away at the back of the larder for my father's birthday in March. This you could call an annual ritual.

Next on mother's list were the Christmas cakes. Three of these— two iced in the traditional manner, and one covered in marzipan only and lightly browned under the grill, for those who didn't like icing.

Then there would be mince pies—the mincemeat entirely home-made—and later on sausage rolls, jellies, trifles and so on. All this was, needless to say, in addition to mother's regular weekly cooking.

There would also be the cooked meats to prepare; often a ham to boil, usually a tongue—pressed in a round cake tin, with a flat iron on top—and always a large joint of pressed beef. This would be ordered from the butcher several weeks before Christmas. He would pickle it in brine before delivering it and we would have to soak it in water for two or three days before boiling it for several hours. It was really delicious and was laid out on the table on Christmas morning, together with bread, butter and plates of fruit. We didn't have a set breakfast that day. Some of us would have been up till the early hours, making final preparations, and people would be coming down at all different times, so everybody just helped themselves to what they wanted.

My father's entrance on Christmas morning was always a special moment. He adored Christmas and all his life continued to hang up a stocking on Christmas Eve. As youngsters we would stuff our presents for him in it (although, when very young, it never occurred to us that if *we* filled *his* stocking, perhaps *he* filled *ours* after we were asleep; *that* , we knew, was done by Father Christmas). When older we would usually play some trick, such as drawing a face on a white balloon, putting a beret on it, fastening it with a scarf to his walking stick and standing it up at the bottom of the bed, so it was the first thing he saw when he awoke.

Father would slowly open his presents and meticulously enter each one in his notebook, together with the name of the giver, so that he would be sure to thank everybody properly. When he dressed, all those gifts that he could conceivably put on or drape about himself he would. Thus, he might come down wearing three or four ties, gloves, a pullover and a cardigan, one each from two pairs of socks, carrying a couple of books, and with items like wallets, pocket knives or pens hanging by string from his buttons.

For us girls the morning was mostly given over to helping mother get the Christmas dinner—cooking the turkey, preparing the vegetables, warming up the Christmas pudding, making the white sauce, and so on.

After a fairly somnolent afternoon and a light tea, our evening would be given over to games of every kind—more boisterous ones when we were younger, then later on, paper games such as Telegrams and Consequences. The evening usually ended with the singing of old songs and carols round the piano.

Finally, when it seemed the party was about to break up, my father would wait for a suitable moment and then say quietly:

'Let's have a short word of prayer, shall we?'

Wherever we happened to be, we would kneel down and he would offer up a short prayer of thanksgiving for the day.

After this our parents would take themselves off to bed, though the young people usually stayed up for several more hours, eating, drinking, telling stories or just talking. It was always the early hours before the last light went out.

And that was only the start of our Christmas celebrations, for the next few days would be spent in a whirl of family visits. My mother's three sisters were all married, with children, and each day three families would descend on the house of the fourth. A cab or cabs would come for us after lunch and off we would troop. We enjoyed all the visits in different ways. Aunt Bess, for instance, had huge wardrobes and chests full of clothes, of which we were given complete freedom, and we had the most wonderful charades, spending ages dressing up in the most bizarre ways. Both Aunt Annie and Aunt Mim had very big houses, with long corridors, which, when we were little, were absolutely marvellous for hide and seek. The games seemed to go on for hours, with even Uncle Archie sometimes joining in.

Uncle Archie was Aunt Annie's husband (they were the parents of Cyril, who supplied the money for the seaman's trousers)—a kindly but unworldly Scotsman from Dundee. He was just about the most devout person I've ever met, making even Mrs Lipscome appear worldly. Although he was a successful businessman running his own printing and rubber stamp manufacturing works (his samples always carrying not the conventional business phrases, but Biblical texts), he really seemed, away from the office, to have no interests apart from his religion. However, once a year he could be persuaded to unbend a little for some games with the children. He always discovered the most incredible places to hide, even in other people's houses, and was invariably the last to be found, tucked into some corner you'd think would not hold a child—and usually reading his pocket New Testament, by the light of a small torch.

It was Uncle Archie who was responsible for what was nearly a Christmas tragedy of unprecedented proportions.

Young children were not to be allowed to get over-heated, and after a strenuous game, we had to rest for a while. So Uncle Archie would read to us. On this occasion about eight of us were seated in rows on a couple of big sofas and Uncle Archie got out a copy of a book called "Wee McGregor". He had a broad Scottish accent, which in those days I found it almost impossible to understand at the best of times. So the effect of his reading was always rather soporific. But this time it was even more so than usual. I just could not keep my eyes open, or, after a few minutes, even sit upright; the room was going round and I felt sick—too sick even to notice that the others were all being affected in the same way. It was only the fortuitous entry of another grown-up, who exclaimed: 'Good heavens—gas!' and immediately hustled us all outside for deep breathing exercises, which saved us. Uncle Archie, engrosed in the exploits of his hero, had quite failed to notice the leak. Even then he seemed a bit puzzled over all the fuss.

The only regular aspect of other people's parties that I found uncomfortable, though, were the suppers. The trouble was that the dining-rooms always seemed terribly cold. One would go, usually immediately after a hectic game, wearing a thin party dress, into an unheated room, and eat a cold supper, ending up with jelly and trifle, which I have always loathed, anyway. Within a few minutes one would be shivering. On the nights we were hosts mother used always to keep a fire blazing in the dining-room and would never fail to serve a partly-hot meal—creamed potatoes with the cold meat, and hot Christmas pudding with white sauce afterwards.

The second party of the Christmas season which we gave was always for the Sunday School teachers. As many as thirty would pile in, and again a big supper, ending with the inevitable Christmas pudding, would be served. (It can be seen that the dozen mother cooked were none too many.) When I was small it always amazed me that people whom one normally saw only on their most proper behaviour could let their hair down so at a Christmas party. Some in fact would go quite crazy and I've known people get positively drunk on nothing stronger than lemonade and sasparella.

Or did my mother add some secret ingredient to those Christmas puddings . . .?

CHAPTER 11

A great deal of one's time in those days seems to have been spent in paying what were merely 'duty' visits on a whole range of relatives and family connections. When I became engaged the number of such calls drastically increased. I had to go with my fiancé to be displayed to all *his* circle of friends and relations. One such family, whom he had been dutifully visiting every six months or so for years, were the Locks. I must admit that I never received a warmer welcome anywhere than at the Locks—nor disliked any visits more.

Mr Locke was a tall, stooping individual, invariably wearing a striped flannel shirt, without a collar or tie, braces, and heavy boots. His favourite saying was: 'I never hurry and I never worry.' His wife was a short, round-faced little woman, shaped just like a cottage loaf. She was always dressed in long black brocade frocks. Their middle-aged unmarried daughter, Pearl, lived with them. She was probably the plainest woman I have ever seen, with a face covered by red patches, and frizzy black hair. Pearl's two great joys in life were a large and malodorous black cat and a scrawny and dirty-looking parrot. (The Locks also had a son, Charlie, who, however, was rarely at home.)

When we arrived at their house the three Locks would all come into the hall to greet us. They were always terribly pleased and excited to see us, hovering around and ushering us like royalty into the parlour. The parrot, in its cage in the corner, would give an angry squawk.

'Listen,' Pearl would say proudly, 'listen to him saying "Hullo, my darling".'

'Sit down, my dear, sit down.' Mrs Lock would lead me to an arm chair. I would lower myself on to it—and immediately a pile of newspapers would be shot out from under the cushion on to the floor. The next couple of minutes would be spent gathering them up and replacing them—farther back on the chair, so that the cushion now tilted forward at an uncomfortable angle and I had to keep my legs braced to avoid sliding off.

Then, as soon as I was finally settled, Pearl's cat would suddenly land with a painful thump on my lap. I never managed to see it before it was there. It seemed to materialize in the air. Nor was I ever ready for it and every time would nearly jump out of my skin.

'Look at that,' Pearl would beam, 'he's really fond of you.' The cat would be digging its claws into my leg prior to settling down for a nap.

'Now.' Mrs Lock and Pearl would sit down in two chairs right opposite me and stare at me. 'Tell us all your news.'

They were insatiable to learn of every minute happening in my life since I'd seen them last, and they would listen, their eyes big, nodding eagerly, saying things like: 'Yes ... yes ... go on ... What happened then? ... Oo, what did he say? ... What did she do? ... Never! ... Go on ...' At first it was flattering, but rapidly became embarrassing.

This was especially the case with Mrs Lock, who had a rather unnerving physical peculiarity. Suddenly her upper eyelid would turn up. It would remain, as it were, inside out for several minutes. If you have never seen this happen to a person you're talking to you cannot imagine how disconcerting it is. I never knew where to look. The strange thing is not that Mrs Lock seemed unconscious of it—perhaps she was—but that Mr Lock and Pearl seemed equally so.

While the two women were hanging upon my every word, Mr Lock would also be listening, but at the same time walking slowly around the room. He wouldn't be *doing* anything, but he would be hardly still for half a minute. He would cross to the window, look out for a few seconds, move to the mantelpiece and stand with his back to it for a moment, walk to the bookcase and stare at the books, turn and go to the table—and so on. If I'd been his wife I would have wanted to scream at him to sit down, but Mrs Lock did not seem even to notice; she was much too interested in finding out what I'd had for supper after getting home from the Whitsun Treat. To me, though, it was extremely unsettling. I would find my eyes being constantly drawn to him and following him around the room, jerk them away, only to find myself confronted by Mrs Lock's inside-out eyelid. At the same time I'd be trying to avoid sliding off the chair and unhooking the cat's claws from my skirt—while being hardly allowed to stop talking for a second. The whole thing going on over the sound of the parrot's incessant screeches in the background. It was all remarkably wearing.

Before very long the Locks would insist on getting a meal. Vain to protest that one didn't really want anything. And useless, too, to vary the hour of one's call to avoid a meal time. Out would come the best china from the cabinet and from a drawer Mrs Lock would take a bright yellow duster and carefully wipe over every piece. The table would be laid and spread with bread and butter, jam, fruit cake, apple tart or whatever. At least, though, I would be able to get out of that chair and dislodge the cat.

I would sit at the table and start on bread and butter. Before I'd eaten a slice, one of the Locks would be passing me the cake.

'Oh, no thank you,' I'd begin, 'I haven't finished my bread and—'

'Well, have a piece now, ready.' And a huge chunk—about an eighth of the cake—would be deposited on my plate.

I would just get to the stage where I'd be cutting a small piece off the edge of the chunk, when an enormous wedge of apple tart would be placed in front of me.

Given half a chance—if all the Locks turned away at the same time for a moment—I'd hastily pass my fiancé a big lump of cake under cover of the table and he'd slip it furtively into his pocket.

Friendly, generous and warm-hearted as they were, I found my visits to the Locks a real burden. 'I think it's that horrible cat I mind most,' I said to my fiancé as we walked home after one visit, while he emptied his pocket of cake. 'I wish it would die!'

On our next visit I noticed that Pearl was very long-faced and it wasn't many minutes after I sat down that I became aware of a welcome absence. 'Er, where's the cat?' I asked hopefully.

'Oh, he's dead,' Mrs Lock said quietly.

'I'm sorry,' I lied. 'How did it happen?'

'It was awful. We left the oven door open and he got in. We didn't know. I shut the door and lit the fire under it.'

Variations of this story have, I understand, become a kind of folk tale, cropping up all over the world; though it is said to be impossible to track down the source. Well, I can certainly vouch for the truth of this one.

'What a ghastly way for that poor cat to die,' I said to my fiancé afterwards. 'But I'm not going to pretend I'm sorry it is gone. I just wish the parrot would die, too—painlessly.'

Next time we called there and were shown into the parlour there was an unusual silence. I looked to the corner where the parrot's cage had stood. It was no longer there.

'Your parrot,' I said. 'Don't say it . . .'

Mrs Lock nodded mournfully. 'Gone. Just dropped dead.'

'Oh dear,' I said slowly.

I felt consumed with guilt. Had I the evil eye? Poor Pearl. Her two joys in life and I felt I'd killed them both.

She seemed so utterly wretched during our entire visit that I found myself thinking momentarily that she looked as though she would be better off . . .

But, no! I fiercely suppressed the thought. I wasn't taking any chances.

The Lock's son, Charlie, was a very different type from his parents and elder sister—studious and quiet. He qualified as a teacher and also took a Sunday School class. One Sunday a boy stayed behind and asked to speak to him.

'Certainly,' Charlie said. 'What about?'

'Me father, sir.'

'Oh, yes? Is there anything wrong?'

'He's awful ill, sir. They say—they say he's dying.'

'I'm very sorry to hear that. Is there something I can do?'

'Could you come and see him, sir?'

'Of course. But are you sure he'd want me to? If he's so sick, will he welcome a total stranger calling on him?'

'Oh yes, sir, he does want you. He asked special.'

'But why should he want to see *me*?'

'Well, he's scared, sir. About dying, like. He wants to know about God and heaven and that sort of thing.'

'I see.' Charlie hesitated. He was good with children but had had no experience at all of ministering to the dying. He felt somewhat nervous. 'Wouldn't it be better if you fetched a vicar or minister?' he asked.

'Not really. He's never been to church, like, but I told him about you and the things you tell us and he said he'd like you to come.'

'Very well. In that case I'll be very . . .' He broke off. He'd been about to say 'pleased', but it hardly seemed an apt word. 'I'll be very privileged to come.'

The following evening Charlie arrived at a small, shabby back street house. He was admitted by the boy, who led him to a dimly-lit room, where a pale-faced man was lying in bed with his eyes closed.

'Oh, is he asleep?' Charlie said, rather relieved. 'Perhaps I'd better call another time . . .'

'No, he's awake.'

How the boy could tell, Charlie didn't know, but he cleared his throat. 'Good evening,' he said to the man in the bed.

The boy looked at him awkwardly. 'No good saying that. He can't hear you.'

'Can't hear me?'

'He's deaf and dumb.'

Charlie's heart sank. How could he get through? Perhaps the man could lip read.

Then the boy added: 'And blind. It was the war.'

Charlie stared at him, horror-stricken. 'Deaf, dumb and blind?' he whispered incredulously. 'Why didn't you warn me?'

'Thought you wouldn't come, sir. People don't like to, when they know. Suppose you'll want to go now?'

'Well, I don't see there's anything . . .' Charlie stopped. He had never felt so helpless. 'I'd like him to know I'm here—that I did come. How do you communicate with him?'

'Sign language. On his arm. A lady taught me how.'

He crossed to the bed and took his father's hand. The man gave a slight start as he did so. The boy began to make lightning movements with his fingers against the man's forearm. After a few seconds the man responded and the boy looked up. 'He says thanks for coming.'

The man raised a hand and made a beckoning motion. Charlie shuffled forward and took the man's hand. He just did not know what to do. Then, like a flash there came to him the famous story of the Prince of Wales and what he had done when faced with a similar situation. He had kissed the patient. Well, thought Charlie, if it's good enough for the Prince of Wales . . . And he bent down and kissed the man gently on the forehead.

Then he found he could not stay in the room another minute. He gave the man's hand a final shake and hurried out to the hall. A few seconds later the boy joined him.

Charlie asked: 'Where's your mother?'

'She's gone,' the boy said.

'Gone? Gone where?'

'Gone away.'

'But who looks after you?'

'Well, me auntie comes in to give us our food and clean up, but she can't spare a lot of time.'

'Doesn't anybody call?'

'Only the doctor.'

'So your father's alone here all day?'

'That's right.'

'But what's he *do*?'

'Nothing. There ain't nothing he can do.'

Charlie took a deep breath. 'This lady who taught you the sign language—where can I get in touch with her?'

During the following weeks Charlie spent every spare minute of his time mastering the complicated method of communication, and it was a proud—though nervous—moment when he next went into that room, took the man's hand and started to 'speak'. The relief when it became clear the man could understand him was tremendous, but the amazement and joy on the man's face was reward enough.

Thereafter, Charlie called on that house nearly every day for several months, gradually explaining to the man all the things he wanted to know.

When eventually the end came for him, his mind was at peace.

This is a story I would never have heard if I hadn't met the Lock family, and I think on consideration it was worth putting up with the cat, the parrot, the cake and the eyelid to have learnt it.

CHAPTER 12

Shortly after I got married, my husband was transferred by his company to a small town in Wiltshire. I had never lived outside Cardiff before and although the town is less than a hundred miles away, I found the change very traumatic.

Firstly, living away from the sea made me feel horribly closed in and claustrophobic—as though everything was crowding in on me. Secondly, I found the people stiffer and not nearly so easy to talk to as in Cardiff. They were polite but it was hard to get to know them. We were to live in that town for a number of years and eventually I made some good friends; but it was tough going at first.

While waiting for a house of our own we lived in a series of lodgings. The first was with a Mrs Burgess. She was a young woman with a baby, but had already got into the habit of addressing her husband—who was about thirty—as 'Daddy'. In spite of this, she seemed quite nice. Our initial shock came at dinner the first evening. None of the food tasted like anything I had ever eaten before. What wasn't totally insipid was quite horrible. It did not take us long to realize the trouble: no salt at all had been used in the cooking. We thought perhaps Mrs Burgess had run short, so we said nothing. But the following days things were no better. Those who have not eaten saltless food cannot imagine what an incredible difference it makes to the taste of things. Eventually we plucked up courage to ask if perhaps we might have some salt in our food.

'Oh no, that's quite impossible,' Mrs Burgess replied. 'I never use salt in my cooking. Daddy doesn't like it.'

I resisted the temptation to say: 'But what about your husband? Doesn't he like it, either?'

We stuck it out for a few weeks at Mrs Burgess's but when one day I discovered on returning from a walk that our room had plainly been searched and our things moved, we decided it was time *we* moved too.

We next went to Mrs Edwards, a bustling, active middle-aged lady. The food was certainly much better here (anything would have been) and we soon settled in.

I mentioned just now returning from a walk. I went for a lot of walks in those days—mostly merely for something to *do*. I had always kept busy but now there was really nothing to occupy me and I was often very bored; there is a limit to the amount of reading one can do. Why I didn't try to get a job I cannot imagine. It just never occurred to either of us that I should. I suppose it was something that in those days young married women simply Did Not Do.

Therefore, being one day at a particularly loose end and seeing Mrs Edwards coming in from the garden with a bowl of runner beans for dinner, I rashly offered to prepare them for her. She was, of course, delighted. I had been taught to trim and slice beans properly, and made a good job of it. The next morning there was a tap on the door of our sitting room. It was Mrs Edwards, carrying another large bowl of beans. 'Ah, my dear, you've done it now,' she said. 'They like your beans much better than mine.' (She had several children and a number of other boarders.) 'You'll have to do them again today.' I did not really mind, but would have liked to be *asked*.

Thereafter, I found myself helping out with some aspect of the cooking every day.

Some time later, Mrs Edwards came up one day to clean our rooms in a great rush, complaining of how much she had to do.

'Well, I'll see to our rooms today, Mrs Edwards,' I said. 'Just leave me the things.'

'Oh, would you, dear? That's so kind.' She dumped her equipment and was gone. I got to work.

The next day I heard a sound on the landing and went out to see Mrs Edwards disappearing down the stairs, having deposited a pile of cleaning equipment—dustpan, brush, polish, dusters, mop—on the floor outside our door. 'You don't mind, do you?' she called, seeing me. 'I've really got so much on.' There seemed little option but to comply.

From then on, as well as helping Mrs Edwards in preparing the meals, I kept our rooms clean and tidy. Again, I did not object—it was something to do—but my husband became quite exasperated. 'Nobody but you,' he said, 'could pay good money for full board and end up doing half the work. Talk about keeping a dog and barking yourself.'

I had to agree and shortly afterwards we took a small flat in the house of a mother and daughter called Wesley, where I could cook and clean without having to pay for the privilege. Mrs Edwards said she was really sorry to see us go, and I'm sure she was.

Miss Wesley was disabled, having lost the use of her legs as a result of meningitis when she was a small girl. She had also had the disease as a baby. 'They should have let me die then,' she told me. 'It always comes back after seven years.' (Actually, I do not believe this to be true.) 'I've never walked since. They had no right to let me live.'

Nevertheless, she seemed to get around the house remarkably well. She had a wheelchair but did not bother to use it indoors, preferring to crawl about and even managing to hump herself upstairs backwards, a step at a time.

Whether Miss Wesley still blamed her mother for letting her live, I don't know, but they were constantly arguing—mostly, it seemed, about cooking. Both had their own firm ideas on this subject and could never agree, Mrs Wesley, for example, liking to add nutmeg to milk puddings, and her daughter refusing to let her.

The arguments continued even when Miss Wesley made one of her fairly infrequent outings. I would hear Mrs Wesley's voice droning on and on, and could not resist going half way down the stairs to listen. She would be rehearsing the next—or perhaps the last—disagreement with her daughter. 'Well, I think that most unreasonable . . . You really must allow me to know best . . . Why don't you let me do it my way just for once?' And so on.

Both ladies were, however, very nice to *us*.

I enjoyed having a kitchen of my own for the first time and did quite a lot of baking. I would often give the Wesleys a dozen Welsh cakes, or whatever it was I had made and occasionally they would reciprocate.

One such time came about a week after we had begun to notice a strange smell in the house. It had seemed to get stronger every day and we had been trying to decide whether to mention it. Then coming into the house one evening we were practically overpowered by it. It was horrible. 'It must be the drains,' I whispered.

At that moment the kitchen door opened, little Mrs Wesley emerged and trotted along the passage towards us. In her hands she carried a large covered tureen. As she drew nearer we suddenly

116

realized that the stench emanated from it. Somehow we refrained from clasping handkerchiefs to our noses.

Mrs Wesley came right up to us, holding out the tureen, like a ritual offering.

'My cousin—a farmer—sent me a hare several weeks ago,' she said. 'We've been hanging it ever since. Today I decided it was ready. For once my daughter allowed me to prepare it just the way I like. Jugged hare and forcemeat balls. Delicious. We kept you some—a little treat.'

My husband gingerly took the tureen from her. Weakly we muttered our thanks and made our way upstairs. 'Eat it while it's hot,' Mrs Wesley called out gaily after us.

Safely in our kitchen, we collapsed in stifled laughter. 'What are we going to do with it?' I gasped. 'I'm not touching it. But we can't just leave it stinking the place out.'

'I'll flush it away, a little at a time,' my husband said. And so he did. For ever afterwards we referred to the contents of that tureen as the Superfluous Hare.

At last I knew why Miss Wesley stopped her mother cooking things as she liked them.

One other incident stands out from our time at the Wesleys. It was Easter and at tea time one day there came a knock at our door. I opened it. It was a nephew of Mrs Wesley, a student, who was staying with them for the holidays. He was carrying a tea plate on which reposed five quite small buns. 'Auntie thought you might care for some hot cross buns,' he said.

'Oh, thank you very much,' I said, starting to take the plate.

He drew back, a look of horror coming to his face. 'Oh, I say, don't take them all! That's all we've got.'

It was all very different from Number Six.

We went into lodgings once more—with a Mrs Restarick, a pleasant, motherly type of lady, who used to run my bath for me. The only trouble there was that everybody was dreadfully polite—all the time. I could always feel the politeness creeping over me when I went in the door. The strain was terrible.

Eventually, to our great relief, we obtained a house of our own. It was just a suburban 'semi' and seemed small after Number Six; but by comparison with our lodgings it was a palace. It was there, shortly before the outbreak of the second war, that my son, Jimmy was born.

My husband at this time was slightly above the age for military service. However, he was determined to do something and when it began to look as though war was inevitable, he volunteered for the Police War Reserve. To his astonishment he was 'called up' on the very day war was declared—a policeman coming to the house in the evening and escorting him to the local station. He felt as though he were under arrest. A number of other volunteers had also been rounded up and were being issued with uniforms. The one my husband was given turned out to be about four sizes too big and must have been made for a giant. The greatcoat reached almost to the floor and the sleeves extended to the ends of his fingers. The Sergeant told him later that when he saw my husband on parade it was all he could do to call out his orders, for fear of laughing.

Having issued the recruits with uniforms, it became clear that the Inspector had no idea what to do with them. However, he eventually found assignments for them all. My husband was sent to guard a large railway bridge on the outskirts of town. To repel saboteurs, he was issued with a standard police truncheon.

This duty went on every night for about three weeks and was the most boring time of his life. To keep awake he used to play cricket with himself—bowling imaginary balls and hitting them for six with an invisible bat. During the whole of that period he received, apart from a little light drilling, no training of any kind.

Then, however, he managed to obtain a transfer to the Auxiliary Fire Service. Here he received a proper training—and a uniform that fitted. The AFS eventually became the National Fire Service and my husband served with it for four and a half years—right through the blitz. He fought fires as far apart as Southampton, Plymouth, Bristol and Cardiff. Except for the fact that the NFS carried no weapons, it was a life as tough and sometimes as dangerous as that faced by many military units, and I think my husband enjoyed every minute of it.

Early in the war we were informed that people with unoccupied bedrooms in their houses would be liable suddenly to have troops billeted on them and that the only way to avoid this was to fill up the rooms as quickly as possible. With my husband in the NFS and away much of the time, I was, apart from my toddler son, alone in the house and was naturally anxious not to have the place filled with soldiers. So we decided that the only thing to do was let the upper floor as a furnished flat.

We went to a great deal of trouble getting the place really nice. Except for bedding, we supplied everything that could be required, including crockery, cutlery and kitchen utensils, table linen and tea cloths. My husband even fitted window boxes. For this we fixed a rental of 18/6 (93p) a week.

Our first tenants were two girls from a local bank. They stayed happily with us for nearly two years until there was a reorganization at the bank and they were told they were to be transferred. They gave us a week's notice and we advertised the flat again, making it clear it would be available in a fortnight. We had a great number of applicants, the most eager being a young engaged couple. They were to be married in a day or two, were then off on a two weeks' honeymoon and were desperate for a place to move into on their return. They were neatly-dressed and the man, whose name was Holland, had a good job in a local munitions factory. We told them they could have the flat and they departed almost incoherent with gratitude.

The girls left at the end of that week and I gave the flat a good turn-out. I also took down the curtains and soaked them in, prior to washing, drying, ironing and replacing them over the next couple of days.

About one o'clock the following morning I was woken by the ringing of the door bell. My husband was away on duty, and immediately fearful of bad news, I jumped out of bed and hurried to the hall.

'Who is it?' I called.

A woman's voice answered. 'It's Mr and Mrs Holland.'

I opened the door and stared at them in amazement. 'What—what do you want?' I asked weakly.

'Can we come in, Mrs Anderson? We've got nowhere to go.'

'But you're not supposed to move in till next week.'

'No, but our money ran out and we had to cut our honeymoon short. Can we stay? We're desperate.'

'There's no bedding,' I protested.

'Oh, we'll manage with our coats.'

119

'And there are no curtains up.'

'That doesn't matter, just for tonight.'

'You've forgotten the black-out,' I said. 'And you can't do *every-thing* in pitch darkness.' Already, I realized, I had given way.

I spent the next hour or two helping the Hollands move in. I scoured the place for blankets and rugs and drawing-pinned them up at the windows. I brought up sticks and coal and lit a fire for them in their living room. I lent them milk and some of my precious ration of tea. I eventually got back to bed at about three o'clock.

The next morning I was up early, to wash, dry and iron the upstairs curtains. By working flat out I managed to get them done by late afternoon and took them upstairs to hang them. The Hollands had gone out early, leaving the place in a shambles: clothes were scattered everywhere; two cups with tea dregs still in them were on the table, Mr Holland's hat resting on one of them; the ashes from the fire were still in the grate. I hung the curtains and went downstairs, telling myself that, after all, it *was* their first day and they *were* still officially on their honeymoon.

But my charitable feelings did not last long. Mrs Holland obviously thought she had found a soft touch. She was constantly borrowing—tea, coffee, milk, sugar, flour; even on occasions small amounts of money. And I, like a fool, never said no.

One day she came downstairs, carrying a cup. 'Oh, Mrs Anderson, a friend of mine in the country gave me a dozen eggs yesterday. When I got home one of them was smashed, but I managed to save most of it. I thought your little boy might like it.' And she proffered the cup.

'No, thank you, Mrs Holland,' I said. 'He's not starving yet.'

One weekend we went home to Cardiff. When we returned on Sunday night the Hollands were out. There was nothing unusual about this; they were nearly always out. You could say it was the best thing about them. But the next morning there was still no sign of them. We went upstairs.

The Hollands had done a flit.

The place needless to say was filthy. We noticed that the large leather easy chair had been pushed up against the wall. The reason was soon obvious: the side now hidden had been burnt completely away. The Hollands had tried the same trick with a favourite flower vase of mine, as I discovered when I turned it round while cleaning the next day: there was a gaping, jagged hole in the side that was now next to the wall.

They had also left owing us a week's rent.

'We must be more careful, next time,' my husband and I agreed, 'and only consider people with references.'

Among the next lot of applicants for the flat, though, were a Mr and Mrs Home, another newly-married couple. They did not have references, because they had never rented accommodation before. However, Mr Home was the son of a well-known local butcher, who owned a number of shops around the town. We agreed that the Homes ought to be 'safe'. (The Hollands had both been newcomers to the town, Mrs Holland, I regret to say, from Wales.) Mr Home was some kind of electrical engineer. His wife was a very plain young woman, who was, however, invariably dressed in the height of fashion; she owned masses of clothes and nearly always wore a bow in her hair, matching the outfit of the day. She was a taciturn type, who rarely spoke. This worried me not at all: Mrs Holland had been all smiles.

The Homes I must say gave very little trouble—quiet when they were in but, like their predecessors, nearly always out. After our experiences at Mrs Edwards' I made it a rule never to go near the flat while they were not there. More fool me.

After about three months the Homes gave their notice. Immediately after they had left, I went up to have a look round, accompanied by my mother-in-law, who happened to be staying with us at the time. The first thing we spotted was that a very nice linen chest I had left on the landing for the tenants' use now had a lining of some sort of black powder, which also seemed to have been trodden into the carpet all around. When we examined the powder closely it was obvious that the Homes had used the chest to store their coal.

That, however, was the least of it. It soon became clear that Mrs Home (who had not had a job) hadn't done a scrap of housework in the whole three months. She could not even have brushed a carpet. I have never before or since seen such dirt. All the empty tins they had lived out of were stacked in one corner of the kitchen, while in another was a

The author with her husband and mother-in-law, 1941.

pile of greasy chip papers; every baking tin and saucepan had been left with putrid food in it.

Crammed into a cabinet drawer I found my lovely linen tablecloths, screwed up into balls, stuck together with dried gravy or sauce. The squalor was indescribable.

As my mother-in-law and I staggered weakly from room to room, uttering low cries of horror, there was a ring at the front door. I went down to answer it and found on the doorstep Mrs Home.

She said: 'Oh, I had to come back. I left my—'

'Do come in, Mrs Home,' I said quietly. 'I wanted to have a word with you.'

I led the way upstairs and to the kitchen. 'Look who's here,' I said to my mother-in-law.

Then I turned on Mrs Home and let fly. I don't remember exactly what I said, but I can on occasions, when my temper is up, be quite blistering and according to my mother-in-law I was so on this occasion. The words 'slut', 'filth', and 'disguisting' figured largely in my vocabulary. I remember holding up the linen tablecloths in front of her face.

Mrs Home remained stony-faced and silent throughout, but then suddenly turned and hurried down the stairs and out of the house, never to be seen again. What it was she had left behind and come back for I never did find out, but anyway she never had it. Small consolation.

Two other things were still to be discovered. When my husband came off duty and was tutting his way around the flat (I left it untouched for him to see), he found that somehow (I never understood the details) Mr Home had tampered with the electrical system and throughout most of their time with us the Homes had been using our power and had spent not a penny of their own on electricity.

But just about the last straw came to light the next day. My mother-in-law absolutely insisted on helping me clean the flat and went up early to make a start, while I was to join her after doing my regular work. But after about ten minutes she came rushing down the stairs, practically in hysterics—half laughing, half crying. She was carrying a dustpan, which she thrust out at me. 'Under the bed,' she gasped.

I peered into the pan. The bottom of it was covered with literally hundreds of nail clippings.

Ugh!

We had one more lot of tenants—a middle-aged couple called Williams. Mr Williams had a job—I forget exactly what—that kept him constantly on the move, all round the country, a few months here, a year or two there. His wife travelled with him and in thirty years of marriage had never had a place of her own. She was a sad, lonely woman. Her husband spent very little time at home; at weekends when not working he would be off fishing from morning till night, and not having the opportunity to make friends, Mrs Williams passed nearly all her time on her own, reading or knitting. She would rarely bother to cook for herself and I used sometimes to take her up a dinner (rations allowing). She was pathetically grateful for such little actions and when the time came for them to move on again she was nearly in tears.

'I've lived in literally dozens of other people's houses,' she said 'Flats and rooms and lodgings. This has been far the nicest. I've been really happy here. I do wish we could stay.'

Which proved, I think, that I was not too bad a landlady. Mrs Williams had done a little to make up for the Hollands and the Homes. But only a little.

And she did nothing at all to make up for the discovery that as a woman whose husband was away at night I would not, after all, have had soldiers billeted on me—and we need not have let the flat in the first place.

'Never again,' I said. 'Never again am I going to have strangers in my house.'

But I spoke too soon.

In 1944 my father died of angina after a long illness. The rest of the family were all married and scattered round the country and my mother, herself now rather frail, was left alone in No. 6. For company more than any other reason, she let rooms to a charming young couple called Godfrey. It soon transpired, however, that Mr Godfrey was a hopeless drunk. He would go every evening to the pub and spent practically all his wages there. He was, though, very well behaved at home, as was his wife, so my mother let them stay. Eventually they were allocated a council house and moved away.

Lydia and Lewis at the time of their Golden Wedding.

It was only then my mother discovered that several pieces of her best silver and most of her good linen had gone with them. She suspected it was *Mrs* Godfrey who had taken them—and probably just in order to live. Typically, she refused to inform the police.

Evidently she could not be allowed to run the risk of the same thing happening again. Nor could she live alone. Much family discussion took place. My brothers and brothers-in-law were all setled in long-established jobs. On the other hand, with the war drawing to a close, it was clear my husband's service with the NFS would soon be over. Moreover, he had no real desire to return to his pre-war employment. We therefore were the obvious ones to return to Cardiff—and to the rather special place.

CHAPTER 13

We soon settled in again. My husband obtained a good post and my mother was overjoyed to have us there. Sadly, however, her health rapidly deteriorated and it quickly became clear that she would either have to go into hospital or have a full-time nurse. We decided on the latter.

Here Uncle Henry enters the picture once more. He turned up at the house one day, accompanied by a strange woman. 'This is Mrs Manfield,' he said. 'She's a first-class nurse. She'll look after your mother.' And he went—leaving me no choice but to take the woman in.

Mrs Manfield was a large, middle-aged person, with a strange way of talking—chewing every word and spitting it out, as though she didn't like the taste. From the start she left me in no doubts as to her requirements, telling me within a few minutes of her arrival: 'I shall need a full pint of milk every morning for my breakfast.' She got it (of course) and so things continued. 'I'll have a cauliflower (or whatever) with my dinner today, and please cut off all the leaves—I only want the white.' Every meal it was the same. Instead of telling her she could have the same as us and like it, I spent hours cooking her special meals, all of which had to be just so, and waiting on her.

A couple of days after she arrived a huge cabin trunk was delivered. It was full of her clothes, which had been in store for several months. She demanded the use of my iron and board and spent the entire after-noon in my kitchen, pressing her things—none of which seemed too clean—and hanging them up to air in every available space. The smell was horrible. I felt I was lucky she had not ordered me to press them for her.

At this time my son became very ill, with an abscess on a gland in the neck—which swelled to about twice its normal size. He was in a great deal of pain and eventually needed an operation to have it lanced. Mrs Manfield cheered me up no end by looking at him and shaking her head grimly. 'I've seen several cases like this,' she said. 'They don't usually recover.' (Needless to say, he did.)

I put up with Mrs Manfield because good nurses were hard to come by—and in spite of everything, she did seem a good nurse.

Then one day I was in the hall when I heard a terrible noise break out from my mother's bedroom overhead. Mrs Manfield was shouting at the top of her voice. I heard the words: 'You dirty slut! Look what you've done! Look at this mess.' I could hear my mother sobbing.

I went up those stairs two at a time. I burst into my mother's room. Mrs Manfield was bending over my mother in the bed, shaking her and still shouting abuse. My mother's 'crime' was obvious: she had spilt a bowl of soup over the bed. As I entered I was just in time to see Mrs Manfield slap my mother sharply across the face.

I have never in my life been so angry. 'How dare you!' I shouted. 'How dare you lay a finger on my mother! You wicked, wicked woman! Get out of this house at once!' I was literally shaking with rage.

Within half an hour Mrs Manfield had gone—cabin trunk and all—and from then on I looked after my mother myself.

Uncle Henry, of course, when he heard the story, uttered not a word of regret.

After my mother died we had the house to ourselves for a while. But for two adults and one small boy—and with domestic help very hard to come by—it was really too big, and we decided eventually to have one more attempt at letting part of it as a flat. This time we were determined to get the right tenants. Our first ones were a pleasant, quiet couple called Gable. The only odd thing about them was that Mr Gable sometimes wore his shoes on the wrong feet. At least, either that or he had shoes specially made with buckles on the *inside* of the instep. However, we did not let that put us off them and were quite sorry when they eventually moved away.

Deciding that perhaps our luck had changed, we advertised the flat again. This time the most suitable applicants were a family by the name of Stoneham, consisting of a man, his wife and her five year old son from an earlier marriage. (Her first husband had been killed in the war.) They were from Birmingham, and when I mentioned this to Mrs Cox, the part-time cleaner I had by then found, her face fell.

'What's the matter?' I asked.

'Oh, Mrs Anderson, you want to watch them. Birmingham people can be awful cheeky.'

Well, every place produces its quota of 'cheeky' people and I have met some charming 'Brummies', but in this instance Mrs Cox's forecast was right: the Stonehams *were* cheeky. They arrived with dozens of boxes, far more than they could get into their flat. I told them that they could store the overflow in the back attic, which was kept for a lumber room. I went up later to find that they had put it all in the front attic, which was my son's playroom. I had to ask them to move it.

Then again, when they had been with us a few months Mrs Stoneham asked if we minded her brother coming for the weekend. We were going away ourselves for a few days (I think it was a bank holiday weekend) and I told Mrs Stoneham that her brother could use our spare bedroom. When we got home I asked her if her brother had enjoyed himself. 'Oh yes,' she said. 'My mother came too, as a matter of fact. We put her in your bedroom. That was OK, wasn't it?' I made it quite plain that it was not OK.

There were several such incidents over the months. However, the Stonehams paid their rent regularly and were cheerful and clean, so we let them stay. Besides, I would have put up with a lot of such behaviour for the sake of Mrs Stoneham's 5 year old son, Pete.

Pete was really an enchanting child, with big blue eyes and a most appealing manner. His step-father, I think, was a little jealous of him and did not take a lot of notice of him (though I do not think was actively cruel) and his upbringing was left almost entirely to his mother—who didn't really seem at all qualified for the job.

Pete was the proverbial holy terror, always up to some mischief—to which his mother's invariable response was a good spanking. Poor Pete was always being beaten—largely because he could never get away with anything. He was the most imaginative of story-tellers, always with a long and most convincing excuse, explanation or alibi for his misdeeds. His mother would hear him out, hands on hips, and then ask fiercely in her strong Birmingham accent: 'Is that the truth or a loi?'

Pete's eyes would fill with tears and his lips would tremble. 'A loi,' he would sob. And, of course, he would get another whacking. On the rare occasions that his reply was 'The troof', he was invariably believed and I wondered how long it would be before he awoke to this fact. However, he failed to do so as long as the Stonehams stayed with us.

I had constant urge to warn Mrs Stoneham against these continual spankings, but as I have always hated people who interfere with the way other people bring up their children, I held my tongue.

Eventually, though, I was forced to intervene. One day I answered the door to find a woman called Mrs Logan on the step. She was a red-haired, bossy, interfering person, who lodged with a fat, jovial Italian lady, a Mrs Giovanni, a neighbour from a few doors away.

'I want to see Mrs Stoneham,' she said grimly.

I called Mrs Stoneham and returned to the rear of the house. However, I could not help hearing what went on between the two women; both had powerful voices.

It seemed that Pete had thrown a stone at Ramo, Mrs Giovanni's little boy and cut him. Mrs Logan was demanding retribution. It was typical of her to get involved. Mrs Giovanni, I knew, believed in letting her children fight their own battles; if Ramo had gone to *her*, she would have stuck a Band-Aid on him and asked why he hadn't thrown a stone back. That would have been the end of the matter.

I heard Mrs Stoneham yell for Pete and a few moments later came the sound of loud recriminations, followed by blows and howls from Pete. I rushed out to the hall. Mrs. Stoneham had thrown Pete face down on to the stairs and was kneeling over him, belabouring him unmercifully with both hands. Her face was white with temper. Mrs Logan, looking somewhat shaken, watched from the doorway.

'Mrs Stoneham!' I shouted. 'That's enough!'

She did not look at me, just hauled Pete to his feet and dragged him, still screaming, upstairs.

I walked to the front door. 'Satisfied?' I asked Mrs Logan, and closed the door. I felt, though, that I could not just leave things like that, so after a moment's hesitation, went upstairs. The sound of Pete's sobs was coming from the living room. I tapped on the door and when there was no reply opened it and went in. Pete was curled up in an easy chair, his face buried in the arm. And Mrs Stoneham was lying face down full length on the sofa—also crying her heart out.

This was quite a surprise, as I had always imagined that such incidents were just part of the day's work for her, forgotten in five minutes. But it was now plain that she was as upset as Pete was.

She looked up at me and tried to say something. 'Why do you do it?' I asked. 'Why do you treat him like this?'

'I—I had to do something. That woman—she expected . . .'

'In the first place, it was nothing to do with her. She's just a busy-body. You don't see Ramo's mother coming round, complaining. She's got more sense.'

'But he's got to learn, Mrs Anderson. I can't control him. And Frank doesn't want to get involved. I just don't know what to do.'

I forget what I said to her altogether. But I did try to persuade her that with a child like Pete all these beatings were not the answer. I think my words had some effect—at least for the time being.

As the weeks passed I had to admit to myself that Mrs Stoneham did have a point. She started leaving Pete in my charge when she went out and there was no doubt he *was* difficult to control.

The main problem was his complete unpredictability. For instance, one day when I was looking after him I had a couple of pounds of peas that needed shelling. They seemed to fascinate Pete, who had not, I think ever seen a pea that hadn't come out of a tin. Spotting, as I supposed, a good way, to keep him occupied, I sat him at the kitchen table with two bowls, one for the peas, one for the empty pods, and showed him how to shell them. He appeared really keen to help and for half an hour was as good as gold. Then, without warning, when the bowl was practically full, he gave a loud 'Whee!', picked it up and turned it upside down on his head. Peas cascaded over the floor. Pete gave me an angelic smile and rushed out to the garden.

'Has he been good?' Mrs Stoneham asked on her return.

'Oh—yes,' I said—hoping she wouldn't ask *me* 'Is that the truth or a loi?'

Pete used to wander into our part of the house at will and I never tried to discourage him. One day he was there, telling me some involved fantasy, while I was laying the table for lunch. I had nearly finished and turned away for a moment, when Pete suddenly grabbed a corner of the cloth and heaved with all his might. The table's contents went flying all over the room. The noise was tremendous.

130

For a few seconds I stood staring at Pete in horror, while he just grinned engagingly at me. Then I heard Mrs Stoneham's voice on the stairs 'Everything all roight?'

It was a temptation but I resisted it. I swallowed. 'Yes, thank you, Mrs Stoneham,' I called out. 'I've had an accident, but nobody's hurt.'

The house next door, which had been occupied by so many eccentrics over the years, was now owned by an elderly, rather deaf widow called Mrs Cantor. She had a small back garden, which included a well-tended flower border against the adjoining wall. Pete, of course, had the freedom of our garden and one day I was working in the kitchen when I saw him clambering up the wall and peering over into Mrs Cantor's. I was just wondering whether to go out and get him down before he fell, when he safely dropped down of his own accord. For a few minutes he vanished from my sight, round the corner of the house, but then he reappeared, carefully carrying half a house brick (a few had been left behind when the wartime Anderson shelter had been demolished). He approached the wall again and I idly wondered what he was up to now. For a moment I thought he was going to stand on the piece of brick to make it easier to climb up. But instead he stood on tip-toe and carefully balanced it on top of the wall, which for the second time he started to climb.

By now I was fascinated. Pete was clearly quite at ease climbing the wall and in no danger of falling, so I let him continue. He reached the top, balanced himself, peered down the far side of the wall, picked up the half-brick in both hand and raised it.

At that moment something clicked in my brain. I realised what, in a few seconds, was going to happen. I went out of that kitchen like a rocket, shot across to the wall, grabbed Pete round the waist and swung him to the ground, the half-brick still in his hands. Then, my heart in my mouth, I peered over the wall. I had been right—and in the nick of time. Old Mrs Cantor was kneeling on a cushion by her flower border, placidly weeding. Pete had been in the act of taking aim at her white head at the very instant I had grabbed him.

I was now in a real quandary. This was obviously very serious and could not just be ignored. Yet if I told his mother it would certainly mean another beating for him. And, on the other hand, Pete had not

131

actually *done* anything wrong: he had not dropped the brick. I believe I had stopped him at the last second. But I could not prove this. Pete would obviously deny that he ever meant to drop the brick and it was just possible that he hadn't. There was no way of finding out—the 'truth or loi' gambit only worked for things he might or might not have already done, not for things he might have been planning to do.

In the end I settled for giving Pete a most severe talking to. I really tried to frighten the wits out of him, by warning him of all the terrible things that would happen to him if he even thought about doing such a thing again. I think I got through to him and extracted a promise from him never to climb the wall in future.

It was not long after this that the Stonehams left us. I often thought about little Pete and wondered how he was getting on. But I heard nothing.

Twenty years passed. And then a crime took place in Cardiff which caused quite a local sensation. A well-known club-owner was shot dead in the course of an armed robbery on his premises. It was not long before the police arrested and charged three young men. Among them was one Peter Stoneham.

I was shattered at the news. And I wondered: had Pete's mother taken my advice and stopped beating him? Or had she carried on? And whichever course she had taken, had it been the wrong one? Unanswerable questions. But I still believe my advice to her was sound.

Pete got life imprisonment. Perhaps by now he has been released. Remembering him as he was, and in spite of everything I cannot help hoping he has.

CHAPTER 14

I would never describe myself as an animal-lover—largely because from my earliest age I was frightened of most of them. (I am assured by Lillian that at the age of about four I came running into the house, sobbing because, as I said, a horse had looked at me.) However, I have at various times learned to love individual dogs and cats, and after Chum—poisoned by Mrs Rolt—the earliest of these was Buller. Buller was an Airdale. He was a real character, who used to go for long jaunts on his own, staying out for hours. He was, I'm afraid, terribly spoilt. I was told by Lizzie Roberts, the maid who was left her employers' house, that she once came along the Esplanade to see my mother, who was a real dog lover, standing on the gate, looking anxiously up and down.

'Lizzie, have you seen Buller?' my mother asked.

'No, I haven't seen him all day.'

'The big fool,' my mother said irritably, 'I've been keeping his dinner hot for hours.'

My father was not too fond of dogs, though even he grew attached to Buller. And he was just as soft a touch for a dog as he was for a human being. If he was having one of his late meals, Buller would rush across and sit down by him as soon as he started, gazing plaintively up at him. My father could not withstand this and within a few minutes would be passing him tit-bits. 'Take this dog away, somebody,' he would plead at last. 'He'll have all my dinner at this rate.'

He abhorred cruelty in any form, and from our youngest days it was drummed into us that we were never to allow any creature to suffer. Even insects had to be killed quickly and cleanly. So much was this instilled into us that my brother Len once had a tremendous fight with a boy he found pulling wings off flies. It is a lesson that has stayed with me all my life and today I cannot even put down ant powder without worrying for hours in case the things are suffering.

After Buller's demise I did not want another dog and in fact had no animals in the house until I was grown up with a child of my own. But my small son was crazy about them and was ever returning home with sick or injured creatures—a dove, a hedgehog, even a mole—all of which were nursed back to health. He had, needless to say, a great number of pets.

The first of these was a goldfish—not a creature, one would think, that could cause a lot of trouble. But ours developed a strange complaint which caused some sort of frothy substance to form over the mouth. My son was frantic, in case it could not eat and died of starvation. Something had to be done. I think my husband is the only person ever to sit up all night, wiping froth from the mouth of a goldfish. (I'm pleased to say the patient made a full recovery.)

Then there was Benny, the rabbit. Benny had a hutch in the garden, but sometimes in the evening my son would bring him into the house. After lolloping round for a bit, Benny would make his way to the rug in front of the fire, yawn, stretch himself out and go fast asleep. I will never forget the expression on the face of a lady visitor, when she realized that what she had at first taken to be a small dog or cat asleep in front of the fire was, in fact, a large, black rabbit. 'How—how very unusual,' she said weakly.

There was a succession of cats. Mogs came to us as a tiny kitten, taken from her mother too young and unable to lap. For several weeks I fed her with an old-fashioned fountain pen filler. At first she could not get the hang of it at all and squirmed so much that at the end of the feed she was saturated with warm milk. The only way I could get her clean was to wash her under the tap—a very gentle stream of tepid water, of course. However, this could obviously not continue, so I made her a bib and tied it round her neck every meal time.

Mogs grew into a fine cat and in the fullness of time presented us with a litter of kittens. We kept them for a few weeks and tried hard to find homes for them, but it proved impossible and eventually my husband was forced to take them to the vet to be put down. My son, however, was so heartbroken that in a weak moment I promised that if Mogs had any more we would keep them.

Cunningly, we fully intended to have the vet ensure that no such thing was possible; but somehow we didn't get around to it and in due course the inevitable occurred. The litter numbered five and, while delightful at first, grew horribly quickly. To make matters worse, my small nephew, who was staying with us, brought home a pathetic and bedraggled stray, saying he didn't think one more would make any difference. We now had seven cats. This being the days before Whiskas and Kit-E-Kat, my husband soon became the best customer at the cat's meat shop, bringing home great parcels of smelly horse-flesh. At feeding time the scene was like the lionhouse at the zoo. At last my son was cajoled into allowing me to go back on my promise of keeping them all—provided we found good homes for them. Event-ually, somehow we managed to dispose of four in this way, and sadly at about the same time Mogs died.

We were now left with two, Blackie and Bim, which we decided to keep. Both were cats of character. Blackie, for instance, always liked to sit on the flat padded arm of an old easy chair; it was about six inches wide and he fitted it perfectly. Then, for some reason, we decided to move our furniture around. Blackie's chair was switched to the other side of the room and replaced by one with polished wooden arms, about an inch and a half wide. But even though the new position of Blackie's chair seemed perfectly satisfactory—just as close to the fire and not in a draught—he was having none of it. He had sat in one part of the room, cat and kitten, since he was so high, and there he meant to stay. So he would laboriously balance himself on the narrow slippery wooden arm of the chair that now occupied that spot, and sit there for hours. You've never seen such an uncomfortable cat. He could not relax for a moment, let alone go to sleep, for the second he did so he would fall off. He would just sit upright, his tail curled around him, staring greenly and reproachfully at us. Eventually we had to move the furniture back again, out of sheer compassion.

Blackie's brother, Bim, on the other hand, was happy to settle down anywhere. He was a really affectionate animal, much less independ-ently-minded than most cats. He was the only one I have ever known who liked to be taken for walks. My son was now going to school and every day Bim would walk to the bus stop with him—about two hundred and fifty yards—wait with him until the bus arrived and then make his way back home. I wonder if it was the atmosphere of that neighbourhood that made the animals that lived there as eccentric as some of the human inhabitants.

My first experience of poultry keeping was as a little girl, when my mother kept a couple of hens in a small run in the back garden at No. 6. Their names were Betty and Belinda. She had thought she would try with just two birds, to start with, and all being well increase to six. (There was not really room for more than this, as she also had a thriving kitchen garden.) The hens produced a few eggs, but she soon decided that given the number of eggs she needed a week, even six hens would not be worth the trouble and expense. So it was decreed that B and B would have to be sacrificed to the greater good.

One day when we got home from school, the chicken run was empty. A day or two later there was roast chicken for dinner. We eyed the bird suspiciously. At last one of us asked:

'Is this Betty or Belinda?'

After that no one wanted any part of that chicken, and with a sigh my mother rose to fry some sausages.

A few days after this she produced some jars of delicious-looking potted meat. But when they were opened the smell of chicken was unmistakable—and once again there were no takers. It would have been like eating a member of the family.

It was probably twenty-five years later that my small son was given two tiny chicks at a farm we visited. One was a reddish yellow and the other pale yellow, so we christened them Orange and Lemon. Sadly Orange departed this life overnight, so to console my son my husband went back to the farm to ask if they could spare another. They gladly obliged, but unfortunately the newcomer was also pale yellow.

'What are you going to name it?' I asked my son. 'You can't call them both "Lemon".'

He thought for a moment. 'What day is it?'

'Tuesday.'

'Then we'll call him Tuesday,' he said. (We had probably been reading *Robinson Crusoe* to him at the time.)

So we were stuck with two birds called Lemon and Tuesday.

They survived into adolescence—and as luck would have it turned out both to be cockerels.

We kept them for a while. They seemed to tolerate each other, but as they grew bigger we could see them developing into deadly rivals. This rivalry at first took the form of early morning crowing contests.

They would perch, one each end, on the back of the garden bench, eyeing each other suspiciously. After a minute one would slowly stand up, stretch its neck and utter an ear-piercing 'cock-a-doodle-do'. Then would settle back down, with a complacent air, casting a sideways glance, as if to say: 'Follow that.'

The trouble was the other one always did and this would go on for quite a while. It was an extremely funny sight, but obviously could not be allowed to continue; so Lemon and Tuesday were returned to the farm from which they had come.

I once heard a farmer say that chickens are stupid, characterless creatures, without a thought in their heads other than food. He should have known, one would think, but I was acquainted with at least one small hen who made that statement seem pretty silly.

After the Second War, with rationing still in force, we decided to make a serious attempt at keeping poultry. So we bought twelve day-old chicks from the market, all apparently alert and thriving. We kept them in a warm, airy box and fondly thought we would soon have twelve laying hens in our garden.

Alas, no.

They fell like nine-pins, in spite of our care, and with monotonous regularity yet another would be found upside down, cold and stiff. Like the ten green bottles, soon there was only one and we waited for her to join the others. But she didn't. She decided to live. We called her Toughy. By the time she had grown into a healthy bird, she was one of the family. We became quite attached to her.

We were still determined, however, to keep hens, rather than just a hen, so we next purchased half a dozen pullets, which were soon established in the garden. Naturally, we put Toughy in with them. She obviously did not like them very much—she probably didn't know what they *were*—but she suffered them and settled down to her new life very well.

However, this was no stupid hen. For much of the day we let the birds run free in the garden, and in the late afternoons Toughy would hop onto the window ledge outside our sitting-room and tap on the pane with her beak. My son would go and open the door, call, 'Come on, then,' and in she would trot. When he sat down she would flutter up onto his shoulder and settle there quite happily for as long as she was allowed to. This got to be quite a regular occurrence.

She obviously liked humans, and was also devoted to Mogs, who took the greatest care of her. Quite a hen with a difference. I never did believe that farmer, anyway. Maybe his chickens were characterless and stupid. Or maybe he just did not have the time to notice.

Of all our animals, I suppose the one of fondest memory is Tim. Tim was a liver and white cocker spaniel. He came to us as a long, waggling, frantically friendly six-months-old and stayed nearly fourteen years.

Tim, too, liked people—or at least the ones we showed *we* liked. On the other hand, he hated animals. He seemed to resent their very existence as an impertinence. When other dogs were around it became advisable to keep him on a leash. But, of course, this was not always possible. I remember once when we were picknicking in the country, with Tim running loose, an Alsatian, at least twice his size,

Tim.

appeared from nowhere and approached to investigate us. Five second later it was in full retreat, its tail between its legs, with Tim snapping at its heels. We were torn between anger, amazement—and admiration. Indeed, when Tim returned, looking decidedly pleased with himself, it was hard to resist a few words of congratulation. But that would only have made him worse.

Tim's deepest hatred, however, was reserved for Toby. Toby was a tortoise, bought by my son in Cardiff market. Indeed, he had to be restrained from buying them all, so intense was his pity for them. They were thrown into a cage, piled on top of each other. He bought the one at the bottom, as that was the one he most pitied. Alas, there was still a bottom one. There is always a bottom one in this sad world.

I tried hard to like that tortoise. I just couldn't. I found him a most repellent little object, with his long shrunken neck and his little beady, cunning eyes. One thing I must say of him, though: he had personality. I often think he must have had Welsh blood in his veins, so temperamental was he. He lived, though, a most happy life with us (I think). He had a nice garden to roam about in and was well-fed.

I had read all sorts of things about tortoises. How that they dig themselves a hole in the winter and pop up in the spring. Ours didn't. He waited to be 'boxed' and put in a cupboard, waking up about six months later, renewed. What a life! Occasionally, he would stampede. It quite frightened us the first time. We thought it was his swan song. But eventually we got to expect it. He would practically gallop round the garden and at last collapse, exhausted. We think he was showing off.

Tim, you would have thought, might have tolerated Toby. After all, the tortoise was utterly harmless. But no. He resented the creature very much. It was such a silly thing to have around. It never said anything, never showed annoyance at being barked at, never did anything, in fact. It was just *there*—a blob. Every time a saucer of bread and milk was mixed for Toby, Tim's hackles would rise and his one object was to get into the garden and eat the stuff first. If it was a lettuce or cabbage leaf Toby was given, Tim would await his opportunity, then seize the leaf and deposit it at the very farthest end of the garden. Toby would sigh and set off after it. Though there would usually be somebody around to retrieve it for him.

One year we decided to take a touring caravan holiday. Tim would, of course, accompany us. But what about Toby? We usually arranged for friends to come in daily and feed him when we went away, but this year they were going on holiday at the same time. We could perhaps put out enough food to keep him going for two weeks; but who would turn him right side up again when he toppled over onto his back—a thing he did with irritating frequency? Eventually, we decided to take him with us and he was provided with a luxurious, moss-lined box.

Our first night away we parked in the Forest of Dean and my husband let Toby out to 'stretch his legs', thinking—not very intelligently, as it turned out—that he would not go far. However, when he looked round a little later to give him his supper, before returning him to his box, Toby had vanished. We searched till dark, but no Toby. We felt terribly remorseful.

Next morning we were up with the lark, looking for Toby, all very gloomy and guilty. Then my son had an idea. I thought it was a bit feeble, but we tried it.

The idea was that inside the caravan I was to mix a saucer of bread and milk, watched by Tim, then take it outside, shutting Tim in. The saucer would be put in the car, where it could not be seen or smelt. My son would then let Tim out, keeping him on the leash. The theory was that Tim would search for Toby, in order to steal his breakfast.

Rarely have I seen Tim so agog, as he watched me mix that bread and milk. He had been quite disgusted when he learnt that Toby was coming on holiday and he was now determined to make quite sure that at least the Blob did not enjoy itself.

We clipped the leash on his collar and let him out. He sniffed around madly for a few seconds, then obviously found a scent and set off in hot pursuit, nose to the ground.

And, believe it or not, he found him. We shall ever know how that tortoise did it, but he had walked nearly a quarter of a mile into the forest, had somehow skirted a large pool and was still walking. It was a terrific relief not to have to go away and leave him there.

Tim must have realized how he had been conned and I don't think ever quite forgave himself.

In the end Toby became too much of a responsibility and we gave him to Chester Zoo, whom we had heard were in the market for tortoises. His rail fare for 200 miles was 1/5d (7p.) and we later had a charming letter from the zoo saying he had settled in nicely. (How, I wondered, could they tell.)

It seemed, though, that Toby was happy. My son, who had had him for five years and now had other things on his mind, was content. I was very happy. And Tim was happiest of all.

CHAPTER 15

'I think I'll get a job,' I said. Just like that—out of the blue.

Except for a couple of months as a junior shorthand typist, shortly after leaving school, I had never had a job. (After this, to my relief, it had been decided that I should stay at home and help my mother). As I was now in my forties, the remark seemed terribly amusing to my husband and son.

This irritated me. When I'd said it, I do not think I had really meant it seriously. But after all, why not? For the first period in my life, I had time on my hands. And although we did not really need the money, it would certainly come in useful.

But would anybody take me on? I had never been clever. Intelligent, yes; but clever, no. (I think there is a difference; at least, to my mind there is.) However, it could do no harm to try. I started to read through the job adverts in the *South Wales Echo*.

It was not long before I spotted one that seemed promising. The local branch of 'an internationally-known company' wanted a senior lady clerk. (This, of course, was before the Sex Discrimination Act.) I thought about it for a bit and sent off an application.

To my surprise, a few days later I received a letter, asking me to attend an interview.

I felt this in itself was a minor triumph and, as I was already having second thoughts about the whole idea, seriously considered ringing up to withdraw my application. But having gone so far, I decided I might as well see it through.

The firm was indeed a famous one. They were manufacturers of electrical goods—let's call them BEI—and their offices were in Mountstuart Square. My husband, who was now humouring my whim, offered to take time off to drive me to the interview.

As I went nervously up the lift I told myself that I only really wanted to prove that I *could* get the job if I so desired. I need not actually take it, even if by some unlikely chance I was offered it.

I was interviewed by a charming man named Motson, who was the local branch manger. I determined to be absolutely honest and kept stressing how ignorant I was of office work, how completely inexperienced. This, however, did not seem to matter, as apparently I would be trained. There was no shorthand or typing involved; the work was mainly copying—the entering of figures on to stock sheets. It sounded thoroughly routine and I wondered why the lucky applicant would require training to do anything so simple.

At last the interview drew to a close. 'Well, Mrs Anderson,' Mr Motson said—and I was fully expecting him to continue: 'We'll let you know.' Instead he went on: 'The job's yours, if you want it.'

I stared at him. 'Do you mean it?'

'Of course. When could you start? Today?'

I stammered that oh no, I couldn't possibly, not so soon, things I had to do . . .

'Next Monday, then?'

I felt utterly terrified at the prospect of what I was letting myself in for, but somehow could not bring myself to say no. So Monday was agreed.

'We'll look forward to seeing you,' he said, 'and by the way, there were fifty-four applicants for this job. I made a short list, of course, but I decided after a few minutes not to bother to see anybody else.'

In a complete daze I returned to the street, where my husband was waiting in the car. 'I've got it,' I told him. 'They want me to start Monday. But I'm not going to, of course. I couldn't.'

After congratulating me, he said: 'You know I was against it from the beginning. But now they've given you the job, you've at least got to start—even if you give your notice in after a few days.'

So the following Monday I duly turned up, petrified, at 9 a.m. I reported to Mr Motson, who took me along to a large room, occupied by seven or eight typewriters and an equal number of girls. I was sorry to find I was going to be in the typing pool, but soon discovered that although *in* it, I was not *of* it, as I had a quite different kind of desk—more of a table, about three feet square, at the end of the room, away from the typewriters. It was now well gone nine and I noticed that none of the girls had started work, but were sitting around, chatting.

Mr Motson introduced me to them and explained that I was the new records clerk. At this I fancied that I saw knowing smirks pass between several of them. Mr Motson called across a tall, thin, rather plain ginger-haired girl. 'This is Shirely,' he said. 'She'll show you just what you have to do.' And he went.

Shirley gave a yawn—she yawned a great deal—went to a cupboard and took out a huge roll of paper. She opened it out and spread it on the desk, which it virtually covered. It was printed with literally hundreds of finely-ruled lines and columns, composing possibly a thousand tiny squares. Down the left were listed all the company's products—everything from torch bulbs upwards, all identified by code numbers; and/or long technical names—things like 'Bi-pin 4ft MGFE/6, Daylight instant start', 'Mes. Asst. Col. Dec. Vi Lamps', 'Prefocus BPF Ref 306RH Drive head'. There were literally hundreds of such items.

'This is what you've got to do,' Shirley explained. It seemed that every day copies of yesterday's invoices from the South Wales region would be brought to me. I would have to decipher the sales clerks' handwriting, identify each product according to the accepted short-hand used, add up the total of each item and enter the figures onto the big sheet. It was essential the sheet was completed every day and taken to Mr Motson for despatch that evening to Head Office.

Put like that the job may seem fairly simple, but it was, in fact, immensely complicated. (I was to learn later that seven people had tried to master the job and none had stuck it for more than a couple of weeks.) I nearly walked out there and then, but the stubbornness that had made me apply in the first place made me determined at least to have a go. But I did wish I had been one of the 'unlucky' fifty-three.

'Well,' asked my husband that evening 'given your notice in?'

'Not yet,' I said, 'but I shall Friday. It's an impossible job.'

By Friday, however, although far from having mastered the work, I did think I was beginning to get the hang of it; or was close to beginning to get the hang of it; or was on the brink of being close to beginning to get the hang of it. I certainly did not want to continue doing the beastly job; but it would be nice, before I left, to be able to say I was the only one of eight people to have mastered it. 'I'll give it one more week,' I said.

Nearly twelve months later I was still at BEI. The work now had—almost—become routine, though still needing care and concentration. I had received a commendation from Head Office—and a rise. (Actually I had found an extra ten shillings in my pay packet one week and, thinking there had been a mistake, had gone to the cashier. 'No, there's no mistake,' I was told. 'The workers have been on strike and won a rise.' I knew there had been a strike, of course, but hadn't had a clue they had been striking for *me*. I felt quite touched.)

I had never once failed to get my sheet completed by five o'clock. My housework had not suffered either, as I'd had to work to a schedule and make better use of my time.

Then it was announced that the Department was being closed, all of its work being transferred to Head Office. I had been made redundant. However, I was called into Mr Motson's office and told that They were so pleased with my work that they were happy to offer me a job at Head Office—in Sheffield. I declined.

I was not altogether sorry that the decision to give up had been made for me, as I was liable to have got stuck in a rut there and I could not, in all truth, say I had enjoyed it. All the same, it had been an experience and I had learned a few things.

The chief of these was what ghastly places typing pools can be, and what a tiny amount of work was actually done in this one at least in the course of a day. The girls had absolutely no interest in their jobs, took no pride in them and couldn't care less about doing them well. All they wanted was the pay packet and to do as little as they could while they were there. All had a burning desire to get home at the earliest possible moment. (This applied, incidentally, just as much to the one German girl amongst them as to the British.)

On a typical day 'work' would start at about ten past nine. It would be accompanied throughout the day by a constant stream of chatter—about their boy friends, their husbands, their houses, their latest outfit, what they did last night, what they had for supper, what they were going to have tonight and tomorrow. It was incredibly boring and inane conversation. During the twelve months I was there I do not recall hearing a single clever, witty or even thoughtful remark.

At ten thirty the girls would take it in turns to go out shopping for elevenses. One would go round all the desks with a notebook, writing down orders; a doughnut, a cream bun, a packet of crisps, what have you. While she was out someone would make the tea in the tiny kitchen. When the girl returned work would stop. Out would come the magazines, the papers, the knitting; the talk would intensify. The break would continue for about half an hour. Then, amid loud sighs at the injustice of it, they would reluctantly return to their typewriters.

On my first day I very nearly committed an unpardonable sin. I stopped work to drink the—rather unpleasant—cup of tea that was brought to me, ate a biscuit and read my paper for ten or fifteen minutes. Then I put the cup aside and my paper away and returned to my 'sheet'. A sudden silence ensued and I glanced up to see everyone staring at me, expressions of incredulity on their faces.

'What are you doing?' somebody asked.

'Just my work,' I said blankly.

'You can't start yet!'

'Why not?'

'You'll spoil it for all of us. If you finish your break so soon, they'll say the rest of us can as well.'

There was nothing for it but to go back to my paper for another quarter of an hour.

The actual making of the tea was a despised chore, as it was considered a menial job, tea having to be taken round to the private offices. The girls used grumblingly to do it in turns. During my second or third week I offered to take my turn. I immediately dropped in their estimation. That anyone could *offer* to make the tea! That day half way through our break one of the young men from the drawing office burst in.

'Who made the tea today?' he asked. (I had not gone into the drawing office—just handed the tray to a chap in the doorway.)

'I did,' I said nervously. 'Why? Was there something wrong?'

'Far from it. It's the first decent cup I've had since I've been here. You couldn't make it always in future, could you?'

So I became official tea maker. I didn't mind. It got me away from the inane chatter. And it was one thing I knew I could do really well.

The day ended officially at five, but by half past four all work would have stopped, the only job remaining being to put the covers on the typewriters. The girls would spend the last half hour titivating themselves in the washroom, returning to stand by their desks for five minutes, waiting for the bell to go. Then it would be on with covers and out of the door, as if it had been a fire bell that had rung.

The only day on which they were not eager to rush away was that of the Christmas party. This was a truly horrible affair. Crate after crate of drink was delivered—all at the firm's expense—and practically everybody took far too much. Some of the middle-aged managerial staff seemed to take a fiendish delight in urging more and more liquor on the girls, continually topping up their glasses. After an hour some of them were in a pitiful condition: several were sick; one was lying across a desk, head in hands, sobbing helplessly; while the mouse-like telephonist became violent and had to be held down to stop her fighting. Mr Motson stayed in his office working throughout and I envied him.

For me the year had been a real eye-opener and at first I was glad to be out of it. But now the work bug had got me. I had mastered the unmasterable job. I had been commended. Perhaps I *was* clever, after all. Maybe I could get a slightly more responsaible position. I started studying the job adverts again.

After a while I saw an opening that seemed suitable. An estate agent needed someone to do general office duties. I answered it and was called for an interview.

No place could have been more different from BEI. The offices were small and dark, at the end of an echoing, stone-floored corridor in a dingy Victorian office block in the centre of Cardiff. Inside it was like something out of Dickens. There were two rooms: an outer general office, divided about five feet from the main door by a wood and frosted glass partition with a small window and a door; and, behind, the manager's private office. The firm had been established over a hundred years and throughout that time I do not think anything had been changed. The furniture—which consisted in the main office of a huge square table, a dining room chair and a high clerk's desk with a stool—was heavy and dark. One wall was lined with shelves containing hundreds of bundles of papers, all tied up with string. There was no filing cabinet. On the table was a pile of massive ledgers, each of which looked as if it would take a strong man to lift. Near these were several old-fashioned pen holders and a box of

The author, with her husband, at the time of their Silver Wedding.

Waverley nibs. I would not have been surprised to see Bob Cratchit sitting in the corner, warming his hands at a candle. There was one 'modern' item in the room—a gigantic Underwood typewriter, that looked as if it could have been made as recently as 1914.

I was interviewed by a surprisingly young and energetic-looking man, named Vernon. I learnt that he was the nephew of the owner, had only recently joined the firm, and would be running it more or less on his own; though his uncle, who had partially retired, would still be coming in now and again—to keep, I surmised, a watchful eye on him. (I was later to meet the uncle, a very courteous and correct old gentleman, but who was, as one of the builders who did work for the firm later put it, 'too mean to spend Sunday.')

The work consisted of just about everything that needed to be done in an office: taking dictation, typing, book-keeping, answering the telephone (oh yes, there *was* a phone), giving particulars of properties, taking rents—the firm acted as agents for a number of large property owners—and again, making the tea.

I explained that although I had learned shorthand years ago, I had never been very good and had forgotten much of it, anyway. But I added that I could probably get by with my own particular brand of abbreviated longhand, mixed with the odd bit of shorthand.

In spite of this, to my delight I got the job. This time, I was told, there had been no fewer than eighty-four applicants. 'But,' Mr Vernon said, 'I liked your letter by far the best.'

Things did not start too auspiciously. On my first morning, Mr Vernon said: 'I'm expecting a Mr Roberts to phone me at ten. I don't want to speak to him yet. So tell him I'm out, will you?'

'No,' I said.

He blinked. 'I beg your pardon?'

'I won't tell him you're out when you're not.'

He looked surprised. 'Oh, I see.' For a moment he seemed at a loss. Then he said: 'All right, I'll actually go out. I'll slip down to the tobacconist and buy a box of matches or something. Will that be all right?'

'Certainly,' I said graciously.

At ten exactly the phone rang. Mr Vernon jumped to his feet, hurried to the door, opened it and stood looking back.

I answered the phone, listened and said: 'Yes, Mr Roberts?'

Mr Vernon vanished and I heard his footsteps hurrying down the corridor. 'I'm sorry, Mr Roberts,' I said, 'Mr Vernon isn't in the office at the moment.'

I'd started as I meant to go on and was never again asked to tell a lie.

Actually, I soon discovered Mr Vernon to be utterly straight and a very nice person, devoted to his wife and two little girls. And I grew to enjoy the job very much.

It was an infinitely more interesting one than that at BEI. For one thing one met the public, people from all corners of the earth, of every conceivable age, type and class. And some weird and wonderful characters there were among them, too.

There was the religious maniac—an elderly woman tenant, who used to dress in the most outrageous clothes: big, old-fashioned hats, decorated with flowers, feathers and sometimes whole birds. She would come to pay her rent and ask to see Mr Vernon. If told he was engaged, she would insist on waiting. There she would sit, her eyes fixed on his door. As soon as she saw it start to open she would jump to her feet, dash into his office and start preaching at him.

'Christians!' he would mutter disgustedly when he had succeeded in getting rid of her. (He had, I learned, been brought up a Baptist, but had long since abandoned his church.)

There was the smartly-dressed, slim lady, a widow, born in Cardiff, but who had lived nearly all her life in America. She came home for an extended visit and rented a furnished house from us. Every time she came to the office she was carrying a large box of chocolates. One day she noticed me glancing at it. 'I eat a pound of these every day,' she said holding up the box. 'They are essential to my health. I just can't bear the thought of not eating a pound a day. I get quite ill if I don't. They're so much better in this country than in the States. I'm going to take a lot back with me.'

One of the reasons for her visit was to purchase a burial plot. 'I want my body brought back home when I die,' she said. At the rate she was going, as my son remarked, that would not be far off. (She never, by the way, offered me a chocolate.)

Among the funniest of sights were Mr and Mrs Butler. I call them that because the man looked and acted so exactly like a stage butler. Tall, thin and attired summer and winter in a tail coat, striped trousers, a wing collar and with a watch chain across his waistcoat, he glided rather than walked. His wife, equally tall and thin, dressed always in heavy black material, skirts sweeping the floor and huge elaborate hats, looked as I remembered my grandmother looking when I was very young. Mrs Butler was a highly 'refayned' person, always with some tale to relate, but much too busy chasing the aitches, in case she lost one, to make it sound interesting.

The Butlers were tenants of a small house in a very respectable street, and called quite frequently to see Mr Vernon. When invited in to wait, Mr Butler would seat his wife in a chair and stand behind it, perfectly still, one hand resting on the back, as if posing for a Victorian photograph.

They were exquisitely polite, suave—and, I thought, quite horrible. It was some time, however, before I obtained any confirmation of this. The house next door to theirs, owned by the same landlord, had been empty for a year or more and the Butlers had got to like it that way. Then it had been let to a very nice young married couple. It was their first house, after several years of living in rooms, and they were thrilled with it. But within a few weeks the young wife turned up at our office in tears. The Butlers, it seemed, were throwing all their garbage over the wall into the newcomers' garden. Every day it would be something different: potato peelings, rotten vegetables and fruit, fish bones, the remains of stews and milk puddings.

The dumping would be done overnight, so the Butlers were never seen doing it; but as the girl pointed out, it couldn't have been anybody else. They had been to see Mrs Butler, who had refused to speak to them and had shut the door in their faces.

'I'm so disappointed,' the girl sobbed. 'We were so happy having a place of our own and now everything's spoilt.'

If it had been up to me I should have told her to throw all the stuff back—with interest. Mr Vernon, however, more cautious, just promised to look into it. He asked the Butlers to the office and put the girl's accusations to them. They, of course, denied it indignantly. 'Well,' Mr Vernon said, 'somebody's doing it and if it carries on I shall have to call in the police to investigate the matter. If I then find that you are responsible, I shall have no hesitation in evicting you.'

The Butlers left in a great huff and apparently nothing more ontoward occurred. Sadly, however, the young wife was now so frightened of them that she did not want to stay there any longer. 'They're terrible people,' she said. 'I lie awake at night, wondering what they're going to do next.'

Mr Vernon promised her the very next house that became vacant and soon they moved. The next tenants reported no trouble with the neighbours, so perhaps the Butlers had learnt their lesson.

Another tenant was W.C. Harris. He was a tiny, wizened, unshaven, dirty little man, practically illiterate, who never wore a collar or tie and whose clothes were always too big for him. W.C., as Mr Vernon always called him, was constantly getting behind with his rent and several times came close to being evicted. However, I advised him that if he just paid *something* every week, even if it was only half a crown, he would be in a much stronger position. He took my advice and thereafter paid regularly.

From a builder we sent to do some work there I learnt that the Harrises had six children and that the only furniture in their living room was one large table. There were no chairs or carpet and at meal times the children used to stand around the table, eating fish and chips out of newspaper with their fingers. They all used to be put to sleep in two big beds. I found myself feeling very sorry for those kids.

Then one cold January day, when I was alone in the office, there was a tap on the glass partition. I answered it and saw W.C. peering up at me. He was accompanied by his wife, a dumpy, pink-faced woman, sportlessly clean but, as our builder had put it, 'definitely not a hundred per cent.'

Before I could say 'good morning', the door to the side of the window burst open and I was engulfed. Within seconds the office seemed to be full of children—all apparently the same age and all looking like the Giles family. They swarmed everywhere, three of them rushing into Mr Vernon's office. They climbed on chairs, chased each other round the table, played with the telephone and the typewriter and grabbed at everything in sight. I was running in circles, ineffectually trying to round them up, when Mr Vernon came in.

'What on earth is going on?' he said.

'Invasion,' I told him.

Together we managed to get the children the right side of the partition again. The strange thing was that during the whole episode neither W.C. nor his wife had uttered a word of reproof or made any attempt to check their offspring, just stood by, smiling at them fondly. I also noticed that the children, although shabby, were all obviously happy and healthy and were well wrapped up against the cold, with balaclava helmets, gloves and thick socks. It transpired, in fact, that the Harrises were the most devoted parents, practically all of their meagre resources being spent on their family.

I remember once, at the time of an appalling child murder, W.C., his voice shaking with emotion, saying to me: 'If anyone laid a finger on any of my kids, I'd kill 'im. I wouldn' 'esitate. I'd kill 'im with me bare 'ands.'

I am sure he would have, too, and thereafter did not feel quite sorry for the Harris children.

CHAPTER 16

The Harris family managed to keep their house, but all our tenants were not so lucky. I remember one man who defaulted on his rent time and again. At last the owner decided enough was enough and instructed us to give him notice. He ignored this and an eviction order was issued.

The next morning the phone rang and when I answered it a voice like somebody sweeping a wet road with a hard brush growled: 'Let me speak to him.'

'Who is that?'

'You know who it is. Put him on.'

I said to Mr Vernon: 'I think it's Rogers.'

He took the phone. 'Hullo?'

'I'm going to kill you,' Rogers growled.

Mr Vernon's eyes bulged. 'What did you say?'

'You heard. You're not getting away with this. You watch out, see. I'm going to get you. And what's more,' he added, in something of an anti-climax, 'I'm going to camp out on that landlord's lawn.'

Mr Vernon put the phone down. He stared at me blankly. 'He says he's going to kill me.'

'Oh, you don't want to take any notice of him,' I said blithely, not having been threatened myself. 'It's just talk.'

He pulled himself together. 'Yes, of course it is. You're quite right. People who threaten to do things never carry them out, do they?'

The following morning there was a call from Rogers' ex-landlord. 'That man Rogers,' he said. 'He's camping on my lawn.'

Mr Vernon gave a gulp. 'What's that?'

'When I got up this morning there was a tent pitched there. He won't go. He says he told you what he was going to do. What do you think I should do?'

'Call the police,' Mr Vernon said.

Half an hour later the landlord rang back. 'I called the police.'

'Did they arrest him?'

'No, he left before they got here. I shan't press charges. I don't think he'll give me any more trouble. He did make one rather odd remark.'

'What was that?'

'That he hadn't forgotten the other thing. That you'd know what he meant.'

Mr Vernon made light of it, but he spent the next few minutes searching through the stationery cupboard, eventually unearthing an ancient round mahogany two-foot ruler that he placed in a handy position on his desk. That evening, very unusually, he left early, before it was dark, leaving me to lock up. The ruler went with him.

About five minutes before closing time I was just checking the books, prior to leaving, when I heard somebody coming into the office. The next moment a huge horrible face appeared the other side of the hatch. I had never seen Rogers but I knew even before he spoke that this was he.

'Where is he?' he growled.

'Who?'

'That man Vernon.'

'I'm afraid he's gone home.'

'Huh! Likely story. He's behind that door, inny?'

'No, he's not. Look, I'll show you.' I crossed the room and pushed open the door of the inner office. 'You see, the light's not even on. He went at four o'clock. But you can come right in and look for yourself, if you still don't believe me.' I hoped devoutly he would not take me up on the offer. Though he could have got in easily enough without being invited, if he had wanted to.

He didn't. He just said: 'I'm gonna kill him.'

'Don't be silly,' I said.

He stared. 'Don't you tell me not to be silly. He deserves to be killed —putting innocent people out on the street.'

'But you're not innocent people. You don't pay your rent. Everybody's got to pay their rent. Things couldn't go on if everyone was like you.'

'But listen—'

'Now, don't go bringing more trouble on yourself by making these stupid threats,' I went on. 'You know perfectly well you aren't going to kill anyone.'

He seemed to deflate like a pricked balloon. 'Oh,' he muttered. 'All right, then.' And he left.

I always felt this was my finest hour.

My worst hour at Vernon's, on the contrary, was undoubtedly the period following the Rent Act of 1957. This affected virtually every tenancy—some rents were raised, some lowered, letting conditions were changed; and none of the tenants seemed to understand it. For about a month we had long queues, stretching the whole length of the corridor, all the people desperate to find out just how they were situated.

Then in the middle of this period, at home one evening, I dropped a kettleful of boiling water all over one leg. I have never known such agony. The doctor was called, put on dressings and told me not to stand for a second longer than was necessary for at least a month. But, of course, I knew I could not leave Mr Vernon to cope alone, so I ignored the doctor's instructions, took just a week off and thereafter went in every day. I spent hour after hour standing by the counter, my bandaged leg throbbing and aching abominably. Somehow I got through it and things returned to relative normality.

Who else do I remember from those days? Mrs Dilly, a quiet little widow, who lived in a small terraced house and who always liked to drop in for a chat. I learnt she had four grown-up children. One son was an executive with an oil company in the Persian Gulf, earned a fabulous salary, lived in a mansion and had about a dozen servants. Her second son had emigrated to America, joined the US Air Force, been posted back to Britain and now spent nearly every weekend with his mother. Her elder daughter had also gone to the United States and was running her own flourishing cosmetics manufacturing business in New York. And her younger daughter, beautiful but, I think, dumb, was a highly successful model in London.

I could not help comparing Mrs Dilly with Mrs Hardy, another little old widow and a devout Roman Catholic. She had had one son, who had been killed in the First World War. Every week since—some forty years—she had paid a shilling to have a candle lit for him in her church. She was quite alone in the world, but nonetheless seemed very happy. One day she came in to complain, rather diffidently, about the state of the floorboards in her house. 'They're dangerous, my dear,' she said. 'If they gave way I could be killed. But I want to live as long as I can and die when I can't help it.'

Another character I would rather not recall was the little woman who had a contract to clean all the telephones in the building. She was highly 'religious', a member of one of those modern, very active, American-based sects. She used to talk non-stop from the moment she came in, changing the subject with bewildering speed. She would be speaking, perhaps, about some new member of her church. 'He's a lovely boy, just been converted, you can see the light of God shining in his eyes, that bitch in the office next door said I couldn't do her phone today, she was too busy, well I said to myself, b----- her, if that's the way she wants it, our minister was saying last Sunday . . .' And so on.

'Christians!' Mr Vernon would mutter when she had gone.

Naturally, I remember Mr Smith, a bachelor—polite, withdrawn, rather aloof—who rented a pleasant flat overlooking the river. Soon after new tenants moved into the other part of the house, Mr Smith disappeared. Several weeks passed and then parts of Mr Smith's dismembered body started to be washed up on the river banks. The new tenants were eventually arrested and convicted of his murder. The motive had been robbery.

I could—unfortunately—never forget Mr Summer, about the nastiest man I ever met. As I remarked at the time, he looked like a big fat jelly baby someone had sucked. He was a nurse, then in the geriatric ward, who used to joke about how he would throw the patients around. It was through Mr Summer that I discovered a strange fact: that it is often possible to tell people exactly what you think of them, and get away with it; they will just not take you seriously. My sister Mick used to do it with Lena but I never realized it would work with ordinary people. 'You're horrible,' I said to Summer once, when he was describing how one old man had nearly bounced on to the floor when thrown onto his bed. 'You ought to be sacked. I've a good mind to report you.' He left, chuckling merrily.

On another occasion he was proudly recounting how he had roused his teenage daughter in the middle of the night and brought her downstairs to remove a lipstick she had dared to leave on the mantelpiece. 'You don't deserve a nice family like yours,' I told him. 'Why your wife hasn't left you years ago I don't know.' He thought this hugely funny. 'I mean it,' I insisted. Which only made the joke better.

Summer used to delight in arriving as early as possible to pay his rent and would always be waiting in the corridor when I arrived. 'Late!' he would crow tirumphantly if I turned up a few minutes after the hour. (Mr Vernon never worried about this, as he knew I would always work late without complaint.) 'If I were your boss, I'd give you the sack,' Summer would add as I opened up.

'You?' I'd say. 'What makes you think I'd work for a disgusting man like you? I'd sooner starve.'

In the end I got quite to look forward to Summer's calls. They enabled me to get so much off my chest.

I remember also the charming Pakistani gentleman, who was looking for a large house and for whom I went to a great deal of trouble. When we eventually got him fixed up he was so grateful that he tried to force £2 on me—I think the only tip I was ever offered. I preened myself on a job well done. The unfortunate sequel was that he let every room in that house separately, each to families of five or six people. The first we knew of it was when he appeared in court, charged under the public health regulations. I felt like an accessory before the fact.

With greater pleasure I recall the lovely little elderly spinster, who lived alone in a huge house, except for about a dozen cats. Her father had been a doctor. He had been dead for nearly forty years and in that time nothing in his surgery had ever been moved. His instruments were laid out in neat rows, his appointments book was open on the desk, and so on. Every day his daughter would dust the room conscientiously and then shut it up again. She owned a number of cottages in rural parts of South Wales, which, when she died, she left to the tenants. She had nobody else.

On first joining the firm I found one fellow-employee. This was Mr Jones, the 72-year-old rent collector. He would spend all day of every day going around on his bike and then in the evening would regularly cycle a further seven or eight miles to play chess. With his father.

When I had been with the business a couple of years, Mike joined us. He was a good-tempered young man, with a nice sense of humour. He was a lapsed Catholic, who as a small boy had been forced by his mother to go to Mass every Sunday. 'Mum,' he had said to her once, 'couldn't we be Protestants? Then we wouldn't have to go to church.'

It was about this time that Mr Vernon invested in a dictaphone. Tape recorders were a rarity then and he took it home in the evening to practise with it and put a few letters on tape ready for me to type the next morning. I did so quite satisfactorily, but at the close of the last letter I suddenly heard a little girl's voice start to speak. It was Mr Vernon's youngest daughter, Helen, then about seven. 'Use our soap powder,' she was saying earnestly. 'It's much better than any of the others. Here is Mrs Vernon, an ordinary housewife. Mrs Vernon, please look at these two shirts. One had been washed in our powder and the other in Brand X. Will you point at the one you think is the whitest.' There was a pause, then: 'Oh, Mrs Vernon, what *have* you done?'

I got to know and like all the Vernon family. Mrs Vernon was one of those people, like our evangelist friend Mr Haley, who are continually struggling with a weight problem, always going on to diets and coming off them again. 'Do you know,' she said to me sadly one day. 'I've just been counting my calories and all I can eat for the rest of the week is one aubergine.'

Mr Vernon was a man of simple pleasures, who could go home quite excited of an evening because there were to be 'bangers' for supper. In spite, too, of having abandoned his religion, he loved hymn-singing, particularly the Salvation Army, with their tanbourines. 'Great TV programmes next Sunday,' he said to me one Friday. 'The Sally Army and then Shirely Bassey. Super.'

He had a strange attitude to religion. He was, he said, looking for something to believe in. 'I think it's important that everybody should have something to worship,' he said. 'It doesn't matter what; it can be the sun, for instance. Just so long as there's *something*.'

'I've never heard such nonsense,' I told him. 'That you, brought up as a Baptist, could think it's all right to be a sun-worshipper! Your mother would be ashamed of you.'

On the whole, though, I preferred his attitude and behaviour to that of somebody else I met while working for Vernon's. This was one of the firm's clients, a man called Eddie Peters.

Eddie was a Londoner, long settled in Cardiff. He was a charming individual, plump, pleasant and always smiling. He reminded me irresistably of a drawing of a beaming Christmas pudding in a children's comic. He worked in the office of an insurance company and was a pillar of the Church. During the time I knew him he became, to his great pride, a church warden and by tradition began to sit in the front pew. From the way he talked, I don't think he ever missed a service in that church. But for all this he was, shall we say, extremely fond of money.

Eddie's hobby—and a highly lucrative one—was buying houses. By the time I joined Vernon's he owned half a dozen. We acted as his agents in most of his dealings with his tenants—that is, in his fair dealings. At other times he used another, newly-established firm, which was run by a friend of his named Thomas.

The Wrights were also regular church- (or rather chapel-) goers—members of the same sect as our telephone cleaner. The legal circumstances which led to the trouble between Eddie and the Wrights were complicated but I believe were as follows. The Wrights rented a leasehold house owned by another of our clients, a gentleman called Jenkins. Mrs Wright called at the office every week to pay the rent. The lease on the property had nearly expired and when this happened it would revert to the lessors—i.e., the owners of the land—unless Mr Jenkins purchased the freehold from them. And the law stated that as the leaseholder he had to be given the right to do this. However, Mr Jenkins, who lived several hundred miles away, was elderly and not at all well. Moreover, he was very comfortably off and just did not want to be bothered any more with all the worries of property owning.

Now Eddie Peters somehow found out about the situation—and he coveted the house. It was in a good position, with great potential for improvement and one day could be worth a lot of money. So, by-passing us, he wrote to Mr Jenkins, asking for his permission to approach the lessors (a company called Glamorgan Properties) with a view to purchasing the freehold. Mr Jenkins, though, did not consider this fair to the Wrights. If *they* were to purchase the freehold the house would become theirs just for the price of the land. Otherwise, while they could not be evicted, they would have to go on paying rent ad infinitum. Let them be given first refusal, wrote Mr

Jenkins, and if they turned it down Eddie could go ahead. Ethically, in this situation, Eddie or Thomas his agent, should have written to the Wrights, explaining the position to them and advising them to get legal advice. This is the course Mr Vernon would have followed. Eddie, however, realized that if this were done the Wrights would certainly jump at the chance to own their home. So he hatched a plot.

Firstly, Thomas called at the Wright's house, introduced himself as an estate agent and said he had heard they might be interested in selling their house. They explained that the house was owned by Mr Jenkins. Thomas apologised, thanked them and left. Next, he replied to Jenkins on Eddie's behalf, saying he would put the proposition to the Wrights. Then a week or so later he went to the Wright's street at about the time they would be getting back from chapel. There he 'just happened' to meet them. He made small talk for a minute or two and told them he had been in touch with Mr Jenkins. 'Did you know,' he added, 'that his lease expires soon? So he won't be your landlord any longer. It'll be a firm called Glamorgan Properties, I believe.'

'Won't make any difference to us, will it?' asked Mrs Wright. 'They can't evict us, or anything?'

'No, no, you're prefectly safe. And even if they should sell to somebody else you'd still be OK.'

'Are they thinking of doing that, do you know?' Mr Wright asked.

'Why—not thinking of making an offer yourself, are you?' Thomas chuckled, as though this was a quite ridiculous idea. It was certainly something that had never occurred to the Wrights.

'That would cost us a pretty penny, wouldn't it?' Mr Wright said.

'Oo, I should say so.' Thomas named an approximate figure. 'Then there'd be legal fees,' he added 'and you'd end up having to do all your own repairs and maintenance into the bargain.'

By putting it to the Wrights in this way Thomas had virtually made certain they would say they were not interested. Whereupon Thomas said good day and left them.

That was it. Thomas could report quite truthfully to Mr Jenkins that the offer had been made and the tenants had turned it down. Eddie was then able to buy the freehold himself. The Wrights had been well and truly conned.

I recall vividly the next act of the drama which began with Mrs

Wright, practically demented with rage, storming into the office one day after discovering the truth. Having paid her rent to us for years she at first naturally thought we were involved in the trick. Mr Vernon at last convinced her that her quarrel was solely with Eddie Peters, but there was no calming her.

'He won't get away with it, mister,' she shouted at Mr Vernon. 'The Lord's on our side. You'll see.'

'I'd find it a lot easier to feel sympathy for her,' Mr Vernon sighed after she had gone, 'if only she wouldn't call me "mister".'

The following Sunday Mr Wright skipped morning service at his chapel, in order to wait outside Eddie's church and waylay him when he came out. A furious row erupted, which ended in Wright physically attacking Eddie, who had to be rescued by fellow-worshippers and hustled back into the church for sanctuary.

'Christians!' Mr Vernon muttered disgustedly and predictably when he heard about it.

The Wrights protests were all to no avail, of course. It seemed the Lord had not been on their side. Though I did not feel He could have been on Eddie's either.

I decided to tell Eddie so. 'Fine church warden you are,' I said to him when he next came to the office. 'I should think if you could be a warden anybody could be.'

Mr Vernon was present at the time and positively froze. But Eddie reacted no differently from the way Mr Summer had. If anything he looked as if I had paid him a compliment.

'I don't know how you get away with it,' Mr Vernon said wonderingly, after Eddie had left. 'If *I* said that to him he'd take all his business away—not just the dodgy bits.'

He did not, though, take his business away and was, in fact, quite well-behaved for a while—though later on he was to try another stunt.

Before that, however, I was able to score a point off Mr Vernon. It happened when the young daughter of one of our regular builders—the one who had visited the Harrises—fell seriously ill. One day he called at the office and as usual we asked how she was getting on. Recovering, he told us.

'I'm not a religious man,' he said, 'but I send her to Sunday School. And d'you know, the Superintendent has called at the house every day to enquire about her. He's a wonderful chap, does a tremendous amount of good. He's a professional man, well off, but so modest and unassuming. He's a real credit to his religion.'

'Which Sunday School is it?' I asked.

'It's the Gospel Hall, just down the road from us.'

'Really?' I said, pricking up my ears. 'What's his name? Perhaps I know him.'

He told me. 'He's my cousin,' I said.

I did not add that forty years before my cousin had donated ten shillings to buy an old sailor a pair of trousers.

When the builder had gone I turned to Mr Vernon. 'Christian,' I said pointedly.

'Fair enough,' he replied.

A few days later I was able to say 'Christian' triumphantly again to Mr Vernon, when a young decorator from our church, whom I had recommended, did such a superb job of work on a house that the client came into the office afterwards, talking ecstatically about never having had such wonderfully clean, quiet and polite workmen in the place before.

I do not suppose these two incidents had any connection with it, but the following Monday Mr Vernon said casually:

'We went to church last night.'

'Oh? How nice. Did you enjoy the service?'

'Yes, very much. But do you know what? In the porch afterwards I sold a house.'

He told me which house. It was one that had been on the books for months.

'There you are, you see,' I said. 'Just shows you should go more often, doesn't it?'

And he did. I won't say he became a very regular church goer, but he and his wife did start to go reasonably frequently. I don't think he sold any more houses in the porch, but I'm sure he always hoped.

It was shortly after this that Eddie Peters got up to his tricks again. Another of his properties was a large house which was divided into two spacious self-contained flats. Both were rented, but then the people in the downstairs flat moved away. Eddie would now have liked to sell the property and obviously would get a much better price if he could offer it with vacant possession. The trouble was that the people upstairs were very happy there and had no intention of leaving. They were an elderly, genteel sort of couple named Harper—proper and rather old-fashioned, who always paid their rent on the dot and gave no trouble to anyone. But they were a thorn in Eddie's side.

'I want them out,' he said to my boss.

'I'm sorry,' Mr Vernon told him. 'There's just no way you can get them out. They're excellent tenants.'

'All right, then. I'll let the downstairs again.'

'Yes, I'm sure that's the best thing do to. Shall I advertise it for you?'

Eddie lowered his voice. 'I thought I might let it to blacks.'

'Oh, very well.' Then Mr Vernon frowned, slight suspicion rising in him. Eddie, he knew, was not the type simply to want to foster good race relations. 'Er, why black people specifically?' he asked.

'Well, you see, the Harpers won't like that will they? They won't want darkies living underneath them—particularly if they're really noisy types. They'll be giving in their notice before you can say Jack Robinson.'

'But you won't be any better off. You'll just have the top flat vacant and the lower one occupied.'

Eddie gave a snigger. 'Only for a little while. You see, I'll let the bottom flat furnished. Then as soon as the Harpers have gone, I'll turf the darkies out. That *is* the law, isn't it? I can give tenants notice any time if the property is furnished?'

'Yes, it is,' Mr Vernon said, 'but I'm afraid I can't have anything to do with this. If you're determined to go through with it, I suggest you get your friend Mr Thomas to help you.'

And this Eddie did. He furnished the ground floor flat—very nicely, too, for he wanted to get as good a rent as possible so long as the tenancy lasted—and Thomas advertised it. Because he could not specify 'blacks only' he had to interview all the applicants and, naturally enough, eventually alighted upon some West Indians. They were two enormous young brothers, with their wives and several children. They were self-employed gravel lorry drivers, with their own trucks. For Eddie's purpose they were ideal: to people like the Harpers, they would no doubt *look* highly intimidating, and with four young adults, plus children, they would certainly be very noisy. They were told the flat was theirs.

It was about a month before Mrs Harper came into the office next. 'This is it,' I thought. 'She's come to give notice. Eddie's won again.'

But to my surprise, she just handed over a month's rent. I entered it in the book and as she was about to leave could not resist asking: 'How are you getting on with your new neighbours?'

'Oh, they're very nice,' she replied. 'So friendly. We get on awfully well. It's such a pleasant change having other people in the house again.'

'And they're not noisy?' I asked delightedly.

'Not at all. They go to bed early. And they work very hard. Those boys must be doing really well. They're buying masses of things. It's quite exciting—every day something new is delivered. I really just don't know where they're putting it all.' And she went happily off.

It was the best moment of my time in that office. But even better was to come. It seemed the new tenants had toured the shops of Cardiff, buying on hire purchase everything they could lay their hands on: televisions, radios, hi-fi systems, fridges, linen, china— even a piano. One night they loaded everything into the two lorries and departed. I was later told they had also taken most of Eddie Peters' furniture with them.

I tried hard not to hope they got away with it.

CHAPTER 17

'If I'd known growing old was so nasty,' I said to my son recently, 'I don't think I would have bothered.'

'You don't recommend it, then?' he said.

'No.'

'At least you've learnt a lot. Haven't you got a message for the world?'

'Not one that the world would want.'

'Well, give it, whether the world wants it or not.'

Just this, then. There are not many essentials in this life. Certainly not a lot of money. Enough to keep one solvent and unworried is all I would ever want. Health, of course, is terribly important. So is a happy home life and a loyal family to see one over the hurdles. And, it goes without saying, an unshakable faith in God. How can people manage without this?

I think, though, that in all the ups and downs and ins and outs we each experience, one of the most priceless treasures is a sense of humour. It can see one through so much. Provided, that is to say, it does not show up in the wrong places, as it is apt to do sometimes. In church, for instance. During a lull in the service one day, my son silently passed me the hymn book. He had marked the title of a hymn in the index to first lines. It read: 'There is a land mine'. I suppose in the good old days when that was written there were no such things as land mines. But it was not the best time to spot that line. (The full sentence in the hymn is: 'There is a land mine eye hath seen'.)

On the other hand, a sense of humour can emerge on the most wonderful occasions. My Aunt 'Mim' was very old and very ill in hospital, having had two major throat operations that had left her temporarily dumb. One morning the doctors came on their rounds while the nurse was giving her a blanket bath, so they decided to see her on their way back. When they returned she was propped up in bed, ready for them. She passed the doctor the slate they had given her to write on. She had chalked on it: 'I may not be beautiful, but I *am* clean.'

The author's son.

They laughed. 'You're beautiful as well,' one said.

Once, while going through a particular bad patch myself—when everything that could go wrong with me at one time seemed to do so— I was grumbling: 'Oh, did anyone ever have so many things the matter with them at one time! I'm like Job.'

'Cheer up, then,' said my son. 'Think of all the lovely camels you're going to end up with.'

I made the mistake of repeating this story to an acquaintance one day, not realizing she had little sense of humour. 'Fond of camels, are you, dear?' she asked. What do you say to something like that?

So many things have been said over the years that can still make me laugh. They form no pattern, make up no longer story, but here, to round things off, are some of them.

One December I was ironing and listening to the radio. Someone was appealing for people to invite students who were unable to go home for the holidays to spend Christmas with them. A minute later my son passed through the room.

'Would you like a student for Christmas?' I asked him.

'No, I think I'd sooner stick to turkey,' he said, without stopping.

The small son of some neighbours was the most badly-behaved child I have ever come across—worse than Pete Stoneham and without his charm. He nearly drove his mother insane with his activities: such as hiding a parcel of lamb chops inside a sofa; or emptying the entire contents of the airing cupboard into the bath and turning on the taps. 'What on earth do you do with a child like that?' I said one day.

'I know what I'd do,' said my nephew, who was staying with us.

'What's that?'

'Stick a feather in his cap and take him duck shooting.'

Something rather less drastic was done by one of my in-laws, whose little boy was making an utter pest of himself when she was turning out the main bedroom one day. Suddenly she lost her temper, grabbed him, thrust him into the huge Victorian wardrobe and slammed the door on him. Seconds later she was horrified by what she had done, but thought she ought not to relent too quickly. However, she stayed close to the wardrobe, listening intently for any sign of panic. But all was silent. After about a minute she could stand it no longer and opened the door.

Her little boy glowered up at her. 'I've spit on your coat,' he said, 'and I've spit on your dress and I've spit on your skirt. And now I'm waiting for more spit.'

And while we're on the subject:

Our friend Jean was once troubled by a stubborn wart on her neck, which she could not get rid of.

'Try fasting spittle,' I suggested.

'What on earth is that?'

'Spit on your finger every morning as soon as you wake up and rub the wart with it. But you must do it before you've had anything to eat or drink.'

'Does it work?'

'Well, it worked for me once. That's all I can say.'

A week later I noticed the wart was no different. 'The cure not working?' I asked.

'I keep forgetting to try it,' she said. 'I don't think of it until I've had a cup of coffee. I know—I'll write something on a card and stand it on the dressing table, so I see it first thing.'

This she did and it succeeded in reminding her.

A few days later she returned to her bedroom later in the morning to see the window cleaner outside. He was staring, utterly bemused at the large piece of card propped up on her dressing table. On it, in bold block capitals, was the single word SPIT.

Did that window cleaner, she often wondered, ever after consider her to be quite insane. (Incidentally, the cure worked.)

'Oo,' said my sister-in-law, when we were out for a drive one summer evening, 'just look at that lovely sunset behind the brewery.'

'Oo,' said her husband, 'just look at that lovely brewery in front of the sunset.'

Another time they went out to dinner at the best hotel in Cardiff. Half way through the meal my sister-in-law looked down and saw to her horror that she was wearing odd shoes.

'Do you think I'm going crazy?' she asked her husband later. 'Are you worried about me?'

The author with Jean.

'Not at all,' he replied. 'I'd only start worrying if you wore odd shoes and thought it didn't matter.'

'Remind me not to go there,' said my nephew, after watching a TV documentary about some appalling part of the world.

'Remind me not to go with you when you don't go,' said my husband.

My nephew picked up the paper. 'Couple Lost in Tyrol Rescued,' he read aloud. 'Why don't they just say "Couple Not Lost in Tyrol"?'

'You said you were going to bed early tonight,' I reminded him.

He looked at his watch. 'It's not early yet,' he said.

'I couldn't sleep last night,' said my friend.

'Why didn't you try counting sheep?' I asked.

'It never works for me,' she replied. 'I always have to stay awake to get the last sheep over the fence.'

'I've been in this office forty years,' said the old clerk.

'Well, look,' said my nephew, 'why don't you slip out for a bite to eat? I'll watch things for half an hour.'

'You know,' said a lady recently. 'I liked the Russians better when they were nasty.'

Notice over a display of fresh rabbits on a butcher's stall at Cardiff Market:

> WATERSHIP DOWN
> You've read the book.
> You've seen the film.
> Now eat the cast.

During the war one would have been overjoyed to find a plentiful supply of rabbits in the shops. There never seemed to be enough of anything to go round—but especially meat. Weekend 'joints' were tiny and one hardly ever had anything extra, except, perhaps, for the occasional sausage.

There were, however, the very rare treats . . .

One day I answered the front door to find our butcher standing on the step. He was carrying a tray on which was something covered with a cloth. He whisked away the cloth—to reveal a sheep's head. This was a bit of a shock as I had never seen a sheep's head off a sheep before.

'I had a few of these, Mrs Anderson,' he said. 'I kept them for my best customers. I thought you'd enjoy it.' And he held it out as though he was awarding me some sort of prize.

'Oh,' I said. Then, recovering myself: 'That's awfully kind of you, Mr Martin. How, er, lovely. Thank you so much.'

I took it into the kitchen, put it on the table and sat down to look at it. After doing this for quite a long time I plucked up courage to examine it more closely. The first thing I discovered was that it had a great many very green teeth. Fearing that any minute it might bite me, I hurriedly put it down and backed away.

A few minutes later my husband came in. 'What on earth is that?' he exclaimed.

'A very precious gift,' I told him. 'Mr Martin thought we'd like it. But I can't possibly eat anything with green teeth.'

I half expected him to say: 'You haven't got green teeth,' and before he could do so I showed him what I meant.

'Oh, that's all right,' he said airily. 'I'll take them out.'

He went to the tool cupboard, returned with a pair of pincers, held the head firmly on the table with one hand, gripped the nearest tooth tightly with the pincers and pulled. Nothing happened. He tried again, exerting more force, but with the same result. He paused for thought. 'Perhaps if I twist . . .' he muttered. He tried but could not get the pincers to grip properly and twist at the same time.

'I know,' he said. 'The pliers.'

He made another journey to the tool cupboard, came back with the pliers and deliberately rolled up his sleeves . . .

During the next quarter of an hour I gradually collapsed with more and more hysterical laughter as my husand, red-faced and sweating, struggled to remove just one tooth from that head. He ended up, no more successfully, using a hammer and chisel.

At last he said: 'Maybe if I took it to the tool cupboard and held it in the vice . . .'

But I'd had enough. 'No,' I gasped, 'I hate it. I don't ever want to see it again. I'm going to give it away.'

I put it on a dish, hurried into the garden and called to my neighbour over the fence. She came bustling out.

'Yes, dear?'

'I was wondering if you could use this,' I said. 'The butcher brought it for us but we don't know what to do with it.'

'Do you mean it?' she gasped, her eyes shining.

'Yes, we'd be glad if you'd take it.'

'Oh, it'll make the most wonderful brawn. Thank you very much for thinking of us.'

She took the head reverently from me.

'Er, what about the teeth ?' I murmured.

'Oh, that's no problem,' she said brightly. 'They'll all fall out in the boiling.'

Mrs Hunt did make some lovely brawn. She gave us a plateful to try. Nonetheless, I did hope Mr Martin didn't have any more kind thoughts.

Seen scrawled in the dust of an extremely dirty white car: 'Also in White.'

And on a travelling Blood Transfusion Service caravan: 'Dracula's Mobile Cafe.'

And on a local signpost before a crossroads, with arrows indicating various villages: another arrow, pointing upwards, and written beside it: 'God.' Truer than he knew, perhaps.

My son was given a new zipped Bible. A friend of his had never seen one before and looked at it, puzzled. 'What's the zip for?' he asked. Then his face cleared. 'Oh, I know,' he said. 'It keeps all the goodness in.'

It was one of the worst-ever winter freeze-ups. The roads and pavements were sheer ice. My husband and I were creeping homewards in the car and were nearly there when we saw a lady, loaded with shopping bags, staggering along the pavement, desperately trying to keep her feet. We stopped and found she lived about half a mile away. 'Get in,' I said to her. 'We'll give you a lift.' It transpired she lived at the bottom of a steep hill and eventually we deposited her outside her front door. 'I'm going to sit by the fire and have a large glass of whisky,' she chattered before thanking us and disappearing inside.

Then our troubles began. There was no way my husband could get the car back up the hill. He tried everything, even attempting to reverse up. The light had gone on in the lady's drawing-room but she did not reappear, even though she must have heard our revving engine and spinning wheels.

Eventually, we had to abandon the car and go home on foot. It took us an hour to get up that hill—clinging to each other, slipping and sliding and frequently going down on our knees. I was in a furious temper when we eventually got home.

'It made me sick!' I fumed to my son. 'To think of her sitting in front of a blazing fire, guzzling whisky, while we went through all that! Just for doing somebody a good turn! Take my advice: don't bother. It's not worth it.'

He nodded thoughtfully. 'If I ever write my autobiography,' he said, 'I shall start it this way: *I have always tried to live by the advice given me by my saintly old mother. "Son," she said, her voice shaking with emotion, "don't ever do anybody a good turn."* '

This is *not* my message to the world.